LONDON

BU\
FO\

No

This book to be RF
below unless a rer
telephone, quotir

17 MAR 1976

7 APR 1976

22 MAY 1976

31 JUL 197

ROCK and STONE CRAFT

ELYSE SOMMER

CROWN PUBLISHERS, INC.
NEW YORK

© 1973 by Elyse Sommer

All rights reserved.
No part of this book may be reproduced
or utilized in any form or by any means, electronic or mechanical,
including photocopying, recording, or by any information storage and retrieval system
without permission in writing from the Publisher.

Inquiries should be addressed to Crown Publishers, Inc.,
419 Park Avenue South, New York, N.Y. 10016.

Library of Congress Catalog Card Number: 72-96661
ISBN: 0-517-503530

Printed in the United States of America

Published simultaneously in Canada by
General Publishing Company Limited

Designed by Ruth Smerechniak

CONTENTS

Foreword and Acknowledgments 5

1

PAINTING ON STONES 7

2

PAINTING ALTERNATIVES 22

3

USEFUL STONES 32

4

STONE ASSEMBLAGES 39

5

SCULPTURE 47

6

MOSAICS 64

7

JEWELRY 70

8

HOLIDAYS AND SPECIAL OCCASIONS 78

9

OWLS AND THE ROCK ARTIST 86

Sources of Supplies 93

Index 95

FOREWORD AND ACKNOWLEDGMENTS

ONE OF THE BEST THINGS ABOUT ROCK CRAFTING IS THAT YOUR BASIC MATERIALS are a gift from nature. On a nice day, with a heavy canvas bag for your rocks, a pair of comfortable walking shoes, and a picnic lunch, the search for materials can be half the fun. The walking and bending involved will do wonders for your health and figure!

Since this book is designed for those who want to create with stones, rather than for the gem and mineral crowd, the examples shown are almost exclusively created with the help of ordinary pebbles, rocks, and slate. Eventually the paths of all rockhounds will cross of course. Many collectors have already discovered the excitement of going beyond tumbling and polishing their finds, to create assemblages and sculptures. These collector-artists will find many interesting ideas here. Many rock craftsmen will discover that less-than-perfect gemstones can be bought very inexpensively at flea markets and mineral shows, and these can be used to give extra dimensions to rock crafting.

Rock hunting grounds abound throughout the country. Beaches, lake edges, and creeks yield rocks smoothed and shaped by the water's action. Construction sites offer good finds since the heavy machinery churns up rocks buried beneath the earth's surface. Mineral dumps are veritable treasure troves; as are rock quarries. Hill sites are rich in slate in its natural or flaked form. The more regular pieces are available from masonry suppliers at very nominal cost.

While this book illustrates many specific techniques and stone projects, you will find yourself going off in many creative directions of your own. The step-by-step photographs and instructions are designed primarily to familiarize you with techniques and methods which can be applied to rocks. The very nature of your basic medium, the stone, will help you develop your own variations of the ideas presented. Even small pebbles tend to vary in shape and texture and thus no two pieces of stone art can ever really be exactly alike.

Whether you try all or just a few of the projects and techniques illustrated in these pages, you will find yourself looking at all natural materials with a new eye. The development of a "seeing eye" is the whole secret of rock crafting.

My sincere thanks to all the artists who share my own enthusiasm for stone as an art medium, and particularly to those who contributed their work to this book. If space permitted, many more examples of rock art could have been shown. Once all you readers who are first launching into this exciting craft get going, there will surely be enough rock art to fill a book many times the size of this one. I only wish I could see all the marvelous things I know you will be creating.

A very special note of thanks to my husband, Mike, who not only contributed his own rock paintings and sculptures, but who took most of the photographs.

Photographs by Mike Sommer and Sheila Harkavy unless otherwise credited. All rock art projects by the author unless otherwise noted.

1

PAINTING ON STONES

Much of our knowledge of the prehistoric culture known as the Stone Age has come to us through the paintings done by the cavemen on the stone walls of their homes. These crude drawings were man's method recording his life-style.

Rock painting was also used as a magical craft to attract and kill game animals. It is probably the oldest form of art in existence. Greek sculpture was a follow-up to rock painting.

While the idea of painting on rocks dates back to 100,000 B.C., the acrylic paints favored by most modern stone painters are definitely a development of the Age of Aquarius. The reason most artists use acrylics is that these plastic water-soluble paints adhere well to all types of stone surfaces. Mixed with a touch of white they can cover the surface of a stone; mixed with water, they can be applied as a thin wash, allowing the natural texture of a stone to show through.

India inks and permanent magic markers are helpful for details. The inks and markers are especially recommended for beginners who often have a bit of trouble making very fine lines with a brush.

Acrylic Paints You Will Need

Acrylics are available in an enormous range of colors and shades, from bright strong colors to subtle modular tones. If you buy a large enough assortment you don't need to do any mixing. However, since mixing one's own colors is half the fun of painting, you will undoubtedly want to experiment in this direction.

Basically you will need just the primary colors: red, yellow, and blue, plus black and white. With the primaries you can mix your own secondary colors: violet, orange, and green. However, to give you enough leeway to use colors straight from the tube and to achieve some interesting tones and shadings of your own, here is a list of recommended colors.

Cadmium red (medium) is a bright red which looks well used straight from the tube, and can turn to various shades of pink with the addition of titanium white. The addition of raw umber or black will give you a range of deeper reds. Cadmium yellow, added to cadmium red, will give you bright orange.

Red oxide or burnt sienna is a good earth color for hair, dark skin tones, tree trunks, and so forth. Mixed with a bit of yellow this will give you tones of gold; with a dab of blue it will turn a deep brown; and with ultramarine blue it will produce a most interesting gray.

Cadmium yellow (medium) is a bright pure yellow when used straight from the tube. Mix it with red for shades of orange, with blues for stunning greens, with burnt sienna or red oxide for a deep rich earth color.

Yellow oxide or yellow ocher is an earthier darker yellow than the cadmium yellow. It mixes well with all the colors suggested for cadmium, but will give deeper, subtler tones.

Ultramarine blue. Varying degrees of white added to this will give you a whole range of light blues; varying degrees of black or umber will give you a range of deep blues. Mixed with yellow, the ultramarine blue will give you a green preferable to most greens straight from the tube.

Acra violet. Although certain shades of red and blue will give you violets and purple, the ultramarine blue and cadmium red recommended here would not give you a very satisfactory mixture. Therefore, unless you want to add to your range of reds and blues, a tube of acra violet would be advisable for any lover of purple.

Cadmium orange is optional since cadmium red and cadmium yellow will give you a lovely orange. However, if you love orange and use it a lot, it would be handy to have a tube from which to squeeze orange pure and simple.

Chrome green or Hooker's green. You'll probably want to tone this down with umber or lighten it with yellow oxide rather than to use from the tube. In view of this, it is probably the most optional color on this recommended list. The greens achieved by mixing yellow and blue are much more subtle and interesting.

Flesh is a nice light pink, handy to have if you paint a lot of roses, cherubs, and pink-cheeked people, and easily mixed by adding a bit of yellow oxide to red.

Paintbrushes You Will Need

Use the best paintbrushes you can afford. Acrylic paints wash out easily with soap and water so that the care required for a long brush life is as easy as rinsing your own hands. Sable brushes are ideal.

Some artists like a whole wardrobe of brushes, both flat and pointed. Three well-chosen brushes are all you really need. A #12 brush which ends in a point is very versatile and can be used for fine details as well as larger strokes. A #7 or #8 brush is a good all-purpose brush. You will want one very fine #1 or #2 brush.

Pens and Markers

Since inks and permanent markers work very well on stone surfaces, these are worth considering as an alternative or additional medium, especially for fine line detailing.

Use only markers which are marked PERMANENT. Use a very fine line tip.

When working with ink, you will find refillable pens ideal. Try out various points to see which are most comfortable for you. I like an ultrafine flexible crow quill point best. Since the stone's surface is hard, you'll have to replace the point fairly often. Black ink is very effective on most stones, but you can use colors. Sepia-colored ink is most handsome for ink-drawn faces.

Painting supplies include good quality brushes, tubes of acrylic paint, as well as India or Rapidograph ink, crow quill pen, and fine line permanent markers. Note that the bottoms of the paint tubes are rolled up. Keeping the ends rolled up as you use your paint is especially important with acrylics to avoid drying in the tube.

Painting Accessories

The best mixing palette you can use is a piece of glass or a plate. Dried, leftover paints can be scraped off easily with a knife, the plate or glass rinsed with warm water.

You will also need two water containers, one for cleaning your brushes, and one for picking up fresh water to keep paints moist. This is especially important for acrylics since they dry very fast. A spray bottle filled with water is also handy for adding a dash of moisture to blobs of paint on your palette.

Keep a can of clear plastic spray or varnish spray at hand so that you can give your finished painting a protective coating.

Painting accessories: glass palette, a container of water to clean brushes and one to moisten. The plastic bottle holds water which can be sprayed onto globs of paint to keep them from drying. Clear spray is used as a protective finish for painted stones.

A very handy painting accessory, especially if you are working with a large stone, is a revolving tray. These are available in all hardware stores.

By setting the stone on top of this, you can easily shift it around as you develop your design.

A turntable is a particularly handy accessory when painting a large stone.

Ready, Set, Paint

All right, so you're one of those people who have never painted. Painting a rock is the best possible way to get started. The stone surface absorbs paint beautifully. It needs no priming other than rinsing and drying. You can paint with opaque acrylics, letting the color cover the stone or that portion of the stone which will have a design. You can thin your paint with water and wash it into the stone, using the natural tone and texture for your shading. The watercolor technique will probably be easier for you if you are a beginner.

To get started, squeeze a blob of the colors you plan to use onto your palette. Dip the tip of your brush in water before picking up the paint. Use the wet tip to mix colors if you are going to do any mixing. Paint in the large areas of color and design first. You can use inks or markers for the outlines and accents and fill in with paint.

If you want to cover the entire stone with color, mix some white with the background color and brush it on. Acrylics dry almost immediately so you can go over color areas or add contrasting colored details right away. Acrylic colors used without thinning cover previous colors completely, so if you make a mistake there's no problem about "erasing" it. You can change the tone of an opaque color by dabbing a wet brush into a color. For example, a pink rose or heart or cheek can turn into a rosy glow with a dab from a wet brush.

Now let's take a look at how different rock painters work.

Most rock painters let the shape and texture of a stone dictate their creative thinking. A bump might suggest a head, a crack a nose or a mouth. A large oval might look like an airplane to one artist, or a pussycat to another. Sometimes an artist has a specific idea in mind and searches for a stone to fit that concept.

Start your rock painting by gathering lots of differently shaped rocks. Rinse your stones in water and dry. Then spread them out on a table. Take each stone in your hand (or put it on a turntable if it's very big) and study it from all angles. What do you see? What does the shape suggest to you? If there's a protrusion, think of how you could work this out as a nose, a hat, a handbag. The oval and round stones which have been worn very smooth by water and which are plentiful along the shore make wonderful personalized paperweights. Shown here are two ideas: A portrait of a pet and a ballet slipper (see color section for sneakers). You could also paint a symbol of a friend's or relative's profession or hobby: an eye for an optometrist or eye doctor, a golf club for a golfer, a nurse's cap, a baseball and bat for a big or little leaguer, and so forth.

These rocks were found on the Maine coast and so an association of their forms with seabirds was natural. Each had a latent "head" and "body" that could easily be revealed with painted eyes, bills, wings, and tails. (Jerry Philips, artist and photograph)

This irregular stone had a lump at the top that had a beveled surface leading to a plateau. The slanted surface immediately suggested a face, with the rest of the lump forming a hood. The hood then suggested a monk's habit. The cane and lantern were added to complete the old man. (Jerry Philips, artist and photograph)

Large egg shapes offer all sorts of possibilities. Susan Vaeth painted this one as a gaily abstract lavender and orange cat. It could be done as an inanimate object, like a modernistic car, a bus, or a plane—or how about a slinky mermaid?

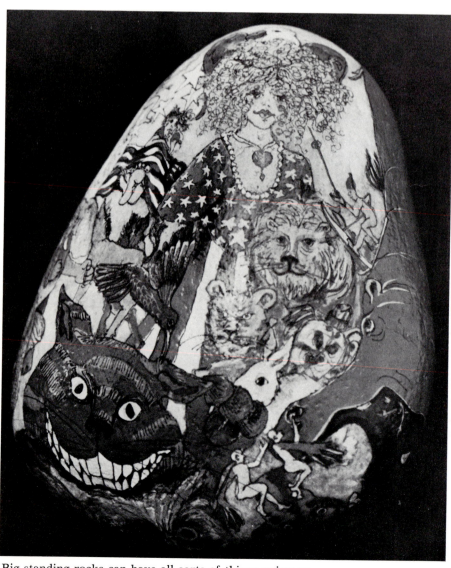

Big standing rocks can have all sorts of things going on all around. (*American Fantasy* by Susan Vaeth)

Two very personalized stones by Frances Scully. The artist spends many hours combing the beach for very smooth foot-shaped stones. In addition to ballet shoes she likes to paint tennis sneakers (see color section) and bare feet.

Florals and landscapes look lovely on smooth stones. They can be used as paperweights, mounted on small easels, or hung as a grouping by cementing picture hooks or beer can rings to the back. (Frances Scully, artist)

ELEGANT STONES

Most semiprecious stones are beautiful in themselves and call for no ornamentation. A collector's quality piece would be too costly to use as a painting surface. However, there are stones which have imperfections: odd shapes and pieces that broke in the process of being slabbed; slabs with imperfect markings or holes. These qualities make the stones less interesting to the collector, and more economically accessible to the rock artist. A little judicious shopping at rock and mineral shows and flea markets can turn up many such low-cost treasures.

Charles Le Norrey has collected a variety of semiprecious stones over the years and his painted stones have become collectors' items for both art and mineral collectors.

When painting on these types of stones never work on a polished surface. Even unpolished stones have an oil finish when the stone is cut or slabbed. Be sure to wash this off with water and dry, or your paint won't adhere.

Some stone slabs are thick enough for the stone to be self-standing. Thinner slabs can be displayed on small easels or attached to clear lucite stands which will show both the front and back. If you use double-sided Scotch tape, even a good-sized slab will stick to the lucite quite firmly and, best of all, invisibly. You will see many more ways of standing, sitting, and hanging your decorated rocks in the pages to come. Rock creations deserve interesting and effective mountings and these ideas can of course be varied to apply to different types of designs.

Geisha girl, dancing with willow on natural black stone from Japan. (Yashikazu Ogino, artist)

Rear view of another stone painted in the Japanese tradition. Lots of gold underscores the elegance of the highly lacquered finish. (Yashikazu Ogino, artist)

Yashikazo Ogino paints elegant geishas, samurais, and other figures in the Japanese tradition on the smooth black stones found mostly in the southern part of Japan. His colors are brilliant, often laced with bits of gold. This artist works mostly with Japanese watercolors but has also used acrylics. To give his stones the luster of oriental lacquer ware, he uses a very modern and American product, Fabulon. This is a hardware store product used to give a hard and durable finish to wooden floors.

Many Japanese gift shops sell these smooth black stones for just a few cents. You might not be able to master the intricacies of Mr. Ogino's delicate designs, but even a simple painting will achieve this elegant oriental look if you use the Fabulon finish.

You might also follow the fine crafts tradition of finishing your stones on the bottom as well as the top. It's always a special sort of esthetic pleasure to pick up something lovely, and find still another artistic surprise. You could let both front and back show, by taping your stone to a lucite stand as already shown.

DOUBLE-SIDED STONE PORTRAITS EMBEDDED IN RESIN

Portraits done on both sides of small stones are lots of fun to do. They could be mounted on pieces of lucite as already shown in the previous

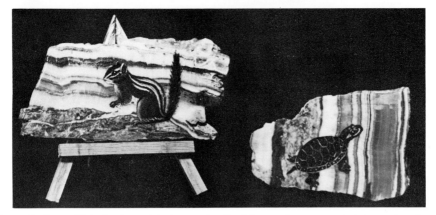

Onyx in beautiful shades of beige and off-white makes a most interesting background for these paintings of a chipmunk and a small turtle. (Charles Le Norrey, artist)

Lucite blocks on which to mount stones come in many shapes. Attach stones with double-sided tape which will hold them securely but can nevertheless be easily removed. *Peace Dove* on blue sodalite stone. (Charles Le Norrey, artist)

pages. One of the most effective ways to display these types of stone portraits is to actually embed them in clear polyester resin which will, with the addition of catalyst or hardener, form a clear plastic block.

Resins come in pint, quart, and gallon cans with enough catalyst provided for the quantity purchased. Although liquid plastic and hardener are easy to handle, it is well to exercise special care in covering work surfaces with thick layers of newspapers and to work in well-ventilated areas. It is best to use only disposable materials for mixing—paper cups, wood sticks, etc. Since resin should be carefully measured and mixed, paper cups with ounce markings are ideal.

While you might find all sorts of usable molds around your kitchen, plastic molds especially made for casting give a smoother finish. Since they are reusable they are well worth the small extra expenditure.

In order to embed a stone in the center of the block, the casting should be done in three stages. Fresh resin and catalyst must be mixed for each of these stages. It will take about thirty minutes for each "pouring" to gel or set. After about ten minutes, the liquid will be thick but still soft. When completely hard you will hear a clicking noise when you tap the surface with a wooden stirrer.

To determine how much resin you need, measure the amount of liquid the mold will hold. For example, the small cube illustrated holds 2½ ounces of liquid. The middle pouring should contain less resin than the bottom and top layers to allow for the space to be taken up by the stone. Thus the 2½ ounces of resin needed to fill the mold will be divided into 1 ounce for the bottom layer, ½ ounce for the middle layer, and 1 ounce for the top layer. The more catalyst you add, the faster the resin will set. I find that for a small cube like this it is best to add 5 drops of hardener to each pouring of resin.

When the final layer of resin and catalyst has hardened, the whole cube will release like a jello mold. It might still be somewhat tacky and it is best to let it cure through for several days. Then, if there are any rough corners or imperfections, you can polish and sand them smooth.

Mix resin and catalyst thoroughly, using disposable paper cup and stirrer. Mix only enough for the first pouring which will fill the bottom third of the mold.

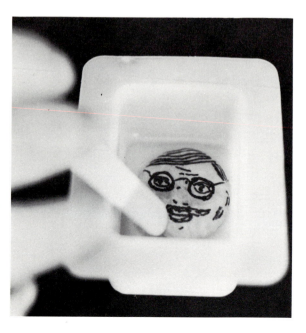

When doing the middle or embedment layer, pour just a tiny bit of the mixture over the first layer and gently set in the stone. This thin anchoring layer will prevent air bubbles from forming. Use a coffee stirrer to hold down the stone which will have a tendency to float to the top end of the mold. If necessary, hold the stone in place with the stirrer while you pour in the rest of the mixture.

After third layer of resin and catalyst have been poured and allowed to harden, the cube is released from the mold simply by holding on to the edges of the mold and pushing the casting out.

The resin embedded portrait has a man on one side; his wife on the other. The painted stone by Susan Vaeth also has a second side and would be a perfect subject for resin casting.

MORE PAINTED STONE IDEAS AND MORE WAYS OF DISPLAYING THEM

The ways stones can be displayed and mounted are indeed almost as varied as the ideas for painting on them. Here are some more ideas for painted stones, each with its own way of sitting or hanging. Stones are glued to the various bases with lots of white glue or 5-minute epoxy, depending upon the artist's preference.

Sleeping Girl. This stone sits quite firmly. It looks charming resting atop the artist's mantel. (Harriette Trifon, artist)

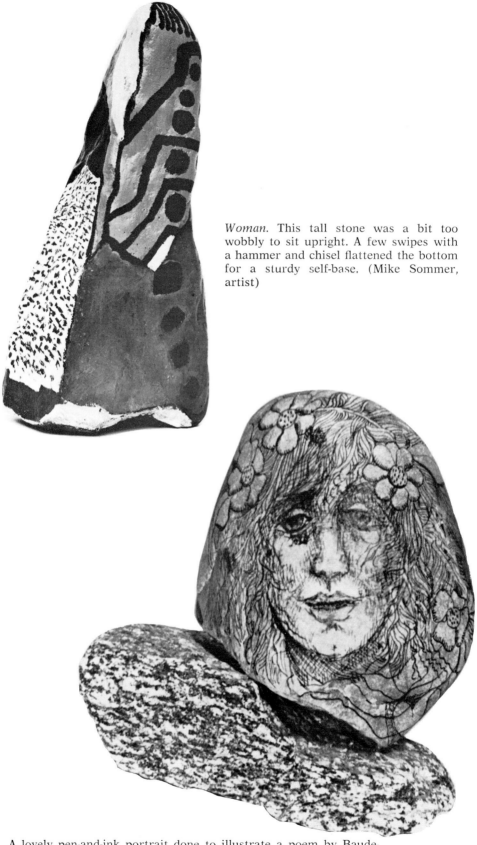

Woman. This tall stone was a bit too wobbly to sit upright. A few swipes with a hammer and chisel flattened the bottom for a sturdy self-base. (Mike Sommer, artist)

A lovely pen-and-ink portrait done to illustrate a poem by Baudelaire which is printed on the back of the head. A smooth stone is needed for this fine pen detail and this combines beautifully with a roughly textured stone base. (Justine Schacter, artist)

Another stone on stone. The base stone in this case was painted green, to provide a grassy habitat for the tawny lion. (Evelyn Meier, artist)

Rock art inspired by Mother Goose. Here Jan Gary painted Simple Simon with a silly grin, red hair, and brilliantly blue eyes, and mounted him on a wooden plaque for hanging. Jack Sprat and his wife make a handsome companion plaque. It took a bit of looking to find the long thin rock that could become a man's full figure but the coast of Belmar, New Jersey, finally provided just the right rock.

Another nursery rhyme by Jan Gary. Since Jack Horner wouldn't be complete without his corner, the artist constructed a corner out of ¼" pine with a floor made from a scrap of tongue and groove oak flooring. The "wall" is covered with miniature wallpaper. Jack himself is a rather brownish rock dressed in green shirt, bright pink shoes, to blend with the wallpaper, and holding a silver spoon and cake tin.

Charles Daugherty and Don Coppola paint rocks as a team. They like Pans. Here's one done on a self-standing stone and another mounted on a gold stand.

White whales of varying sizes, mounted on weathered wood. (Carol Lynn Rosenthal, artist)

2

PAINTING ALTERNATIVES

THERE ARE MANY WAYS TO CREATE DESIGNS WITHOUT USING CONVENTIONAL brush and paint techniques. Let's explore some of the techniques most effective with stone and slate.

Decoupage

When hand-painted furniture became the vogue with seventeenth-century French and Italian nobility, some Venetian cabinetmakers who lacked drawing ability improvised by cutting out the drawings of other artists and pasting them to the furniture. They then embedded these drawings beneath many coats of lacquer so that the effect was that of a hand-painted piece. This method of decorating furniture and objects with cutout papers soon became a popular pastime and in recent years has enjoyed enormous popularity with modern hobbyists.

While decoupage is traditionally associated with boxes and furniture, you will find it an exciting and easy way to decorate rocks and stones. The shapes of the stones lend themselves to all sorts of interesting design possibilities. Stationery, gift wrap papers, old books, and prints can be used for stone decoupage. If you wish, you can combine painting and decoupage by painting background grasses, buildings, bits of sky or sun, and then using a print for the more intricate central motif. Some of the most interesting prints available are black and white, but this should be no deterrent. In fact, the best decoupage is always done with hand-colored prints. Oil colored pencils are fun and easy to use and, if applied with the proper shading and blending, will make prints look like watercolors.

To make a print a permanent part of the rock, apply at least seven coats of a good decoupage finish. A lacquer-based finish dries fast and can be applied every hour. Most varnishes should not be applied more than every eight hours. For a really special finish, the lacquered or varnished rock

Oil colored pencils such as Derwent or Eagle Prismatics, sharpened to a fine point, are the best tools for coloring black and white prints. Use a dark shade in the dark areas of the print, lighter shades in the light areas. A white pencil should be used to blend the colors together for a *painted* look. Be sure to spray your print with clear plastic spray so that your colors don't run when pasted down.

Careful cutting is the key to really good-looking decoupage. Use curved manicure scissors. Cut out the inside parts of the print first. Use the shank of the scissors to cut, letting the points face out, away from the direction in which you are cutting. Wiggle the scissors back and forth to create a serrated knife type of edge which will paste down more smoothly.

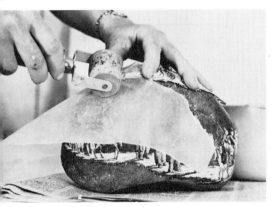 

Glue the cut print carefully with white water soluble glue. Be sure no areas of the print are left without glue or you will have air bubbles. Press the print carefully into any crevices and curves of the rock. After pressing out any excess glue with an almost dry damp sponge, place a piece of wax paper over the pasted-down print and press down all the edges with a small brayer, or the back of a spoon.

After your print has been lacquered or varnished, strips of #320 and #400 sandpaper are dipped in soapy water to rub down the stone, especially the edges of the print. Next the stone is washed, dried, and buffed with pieces of #0000 steel wool, and given a coat of paste wax.

Chinoiserie designs are hand colored and arranged on a large rock to give the effect of figures moving around a mountain. The designs go all around the rock.

should be rubbed down with wet Tri-Mite paper #360 and #400, followed by a dry rubbing with #0000 steel wool and a coat of paste wax. If you like your rocks with a very high sheen, you can skip this final hand rubbing, apply six to eight coats of a high gloss finish, and let it go at that.

Stenciling on Slate and Stone

This popular nineteenth-century craft of brushing color through cutouts becomes a distinctly modern craft when used on smooth stones and slate. Joellen Sommer experimented with various stencils and found masking tape ideal for stone surfaces. The tape adheres to any shape surface firmly and designs can be drawn on with ordinary pencils thus allowing you to erase and make alterations easily. Once you cut around the outlines of the area with an X-Acto knife, you can easily lift and peel away the cut tape. You might design a whole batch of stenciled stones and then save the peeling for something to do while watching TV or relaxing.

Applying color is very easy with this masking tape stencil. Paint won't run underneath even when sprayed. If you want more than one color, you will have to brush it on, of course.

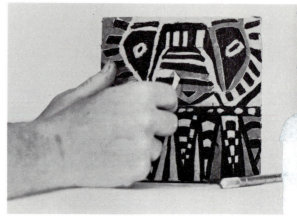

Masking tape stencil design is peeled away after the outline is cut with an X-Acto knife.

Even curved stones can be stenciled if tightly taped.

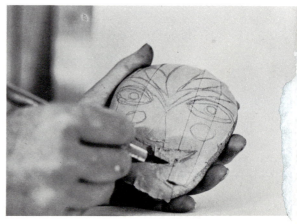

Large red slate with yellow geometric design. These types of designs are very easily achieved with the help of protractors and rulers. A group of these slates could make an attractive modern tabletop. (Joellen Sommer, artist)

A very large and textured stone. The pointy top made for an ideal Harlequin. (Harriette Trifon)

Sunflower mosaic. Beach pebbles embedded into Styrofoam to give uniformity to the surface. (Elyse Sommer)

(Below) A round stone and a plump large one were glued together for this painted duck sculpture. Beaks are hard to find in stone shapes and the tip of an old paintbrush makes a good alternative. The base is petrified wood. (Charles Daugherty and Don Coppola)

Frances Scully's very personalized paperweights range in subject matter from lovely florals to bright sneakers.

Natural pink stones gathered at Rocky Point, Long Island, are used to make a grape still life and a bonsai tree. The grape leaves are bits of conglomerate mineral stone. (Elyse Sommer)

The face and arms of this lovely plump girl were left the natural gray of the stone. (Jan Gary; collection Elyse and Mike Sommer)

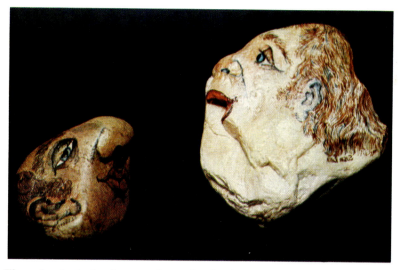

These heads derive interest from the fascinating contours of the stones used. (Susan Vaeth)

Genuine goose egg jewelry box. The edges, frame for the tiny quotation, closing button, and attached stand are all natural pebbles.
(Elyse Sommer)

Engagement Plaque by Arline Shapiro. The happy couple is painted on an antique wooden bellows. The chain of flowers which binds them together is made up of painted stones. (Collection Mr. and Mrs. Robert Andrews)

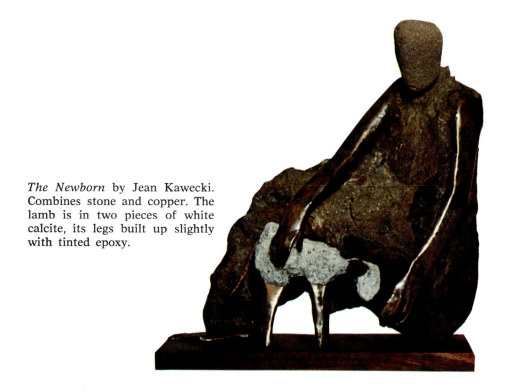

The Newborn by Jean Kawecki. Combines stone and copper. The lamb is in two pieces of white calcite, its legs built up slightly with tinted epoxy.

The natural florid tone of this rock suggested a perfect King Henry VIII to William Gorman. The crown was given a three-dimensional effect with the addition of imitation pearls to each natural peak. Six beach pebbles were painted as queens and glued to the flat back of the rock which was then painted with a regal tapestry background. (Courtesy Karlebach Gallery)

George Washington and Martha by William Gorman. The rock has an uneven crack in one side which seemed to suggest a mouth, unmistakably Washington's. By painting a portrait of Martha on the other side of George, the artist completed this theme: "Behind every great man there stands a woman." (Photo, courtesy artist)

A very special greeting card by Carol Lyn Rosenthal. The heads of the family members and the cat are all painted black stones.

Geisha Girl painted on black stone from Japanese Coast. Lustrous finish is achieved with Fabulon. (Yashikazu Ogiho)

Stones make lovely jewelry. Leaded pendant and belt (Elyse Sommer); pins (Susan Vaeth); lady bug hair barrettes (Carol Lyn Rosenthal).

Painted stones good enough to eat. The pickle slice and tomato are one stone, as are the cheese and bread. The apple is painted on one of the most common shapes found on the shore, a smooth rounded oval. The cucumber and stuffed olives simply demanded to be painted that way. (Jerry Philips; photograph, artist)

A painted stone Noah fitted into a hand-shaped Plexiglas whale by Jerry Philips. (See Chapter 4 for how-to demonstration) (Photograph, artist)

Large river rocks painted with a touch of whimsy. (Mike Sommer)

Jan Gary allowed lots of this elephant's natural rock gray to show through. A wooden base was rough carved to fit the broken bottom, and some shims were used in gluing. The howdah is made with blocks of wood, dowel sticks, and the round wood attachment on top of the howdah is an upholstery tack. The maharajah is a small beach pebble. (Collection Elyse and Mike Sommer)

Owl Monument by William Gorman. The artist, like many others, has been especially attracted to the owl. Over the years he has used literally hundreds of the species as his models. (See Chapter 9 for many owls.) (Photograph, courtesy artist)

Underwater scene painted on an unpolished agate slab. A small hole in the slab makes this collector's "discard" an artist's treasure. (Charles Le Norrey)

Farm scene and giraffe enameled on slate. The background is painted with acrylics. Enameled details give three-dimensional effect. (Walter Vogel)

Hand-colored decoupage against painted sky and earth. (Elyse Sommer)

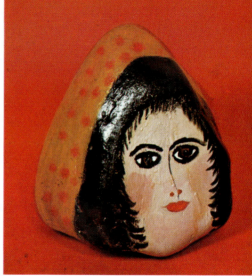

Large river rock painted very primitively with eyes close together to go with the almost grotesque plumpness of the face. The peasant scarf was painted with a carved carrot. (Elyse Sommer)

Trailer Truck by Barton Benesh. (Collection of Seth Allen; photograph © 1970 by The Family Circle, Inc., George Nordhausen, photographer.

Yellow, red, black, and white were brushed into the stencil-cut openings giving this stone the look of a hard-edged painting.

Straw-Blown Ink Designs

Anyone who has seen the delightful accidental shapes and patterns created from Jackson Pollock's drips and dribbles of paints, should enjoy experimenting with straw-blown ink designs on rocks. Smooth-surfaced rocks are best for the ink to run freely. A large rock with interesting all-around contours will allow the ink to travel in many directions to make a varied pattern. Any color ink is usable, though black India ink against a brightly painted stone background seems most effective.

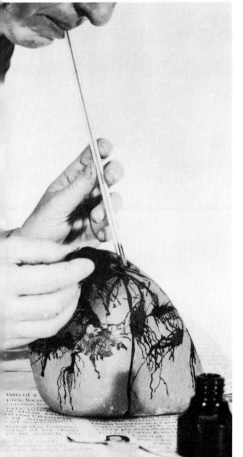

Straw-blown ink design. Black against orange. (Joellen Sommer, artist)

Put a drop of India ink at the top of a rock and blow gently through a straw. Your lips should be curved around the straw. The ink will fan out into thin tendrils, reminiscent of a tree branch. Blow wherever you want the ink to fan out and become thinner. Add more drops of ink and blow some more to complicate the design. A thin brush may be used to thicken and emphasize. Try blowing from the bottom upward.

Spider Webs on Stones

Let nature draw a design on your stones. The beautiful spider web designs shown on this page were created by the orb web builders themselves and collected by Jean Deaton. The best orb spinner is the familiar garden spider. It may spin a three- or four-foot web in two hours. However, since spiders spin their webs only in the summer, this is of necessity a seasonal art.

Here's what you need to catch a spider web:

Large flat stones or pieces of slate, painted black. You can also catch your webs on large pieces of black paper, then cut them apart and mount them on smaller stones as you would a decoupage print.

A can of white spray.

A can of clear plastic spray or clear enamel.

When you see a web you like, apply several coats of white paint carefully. You will be able to see the web more clearly. Now slip your stone carefully behind the web, trying not to break the delicate strands. With clear spray enamel or plastic spray attach the web to the stone. When the sprayed webs have dried thoroughly, apply several more coatings of spray to give the web a permanent protective finish. You can apply varnish or lacquer with a brush for greater luster and thicker protective coating.

Here is Jean Deaton applying white spray paint to better see a web she wants to mount on stone.

These stones are small and only portions of a web could be mounted. Note how the web orb gives the stone at the right the look of a bird. (Webs caught by Jean Deaton)

Enameling

Most contemporary enamelists work on metal, using enameling to add color and decoration. The enameling color is fused to the metal with extremely high heat to give both a high gloss and a durable finish. Neither stone nor slate could withstand the heat of an enameling kiln without cracking.

Walter Vogel, a businessman who became an artist during his retirement years, refused to let this problem of having a stone crack in the conventional enameling process deter him. He wanted to enamel on stone and slate, and so with the typical craftsman's resourcefulness, he invented a polymer type of paint medium which gave the exact effect of an enamel, but which required no heat whatsoever. His charming enamel paintings are the treasured possessions of those who were fortunate enough to buy them while he was still alive and creating. Mr. Vogel's enamel formula died with him. Fortunately for others who would like to try stone enameling, there is a product now available which has the same properties as Mr. Vogel's enamels. This is a polymer color which is mixed with a curing agent or hardener. The mixture dries by air and cures to a tough and shiny finish. A wide variety of colors is available in most hobby shops and these can in turn be mixed to create your own shades.

Enameling, painting, and decoupage are combined in this charming piece. The arrow with the motel sign is cut from a magazine and only the top of the arrow is highlighted with a line of white enamel. Dabs of white enamel are superimposed on the snowy ground to emphasize the feeling of snow-covered mountains. The sky is painted blue. The penguins are white breasted with black wings. The white bodies were put in first, then the black wings and red beaks and feet. One penguin wears a gay green scarf with red dots. These fine line designs are best applied with toothpicks rather than a conventional paintbrush. (Walter Vogel, artist)

One of the most popular forms of enameling is cloisonné. This means that recesses to contain the enamel colors are formed. Usually with narraw strips of metal. The cloisons form little dykes which prevent the enamel colors from running into each other when the enamel is fired. A cloisonné project would be a good way to get your enameling feet wet, since the cloison separations are security blankets that keep you from worrying about colors running into one another.

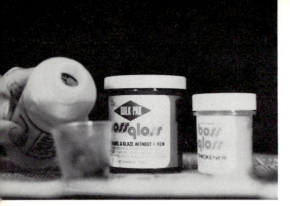 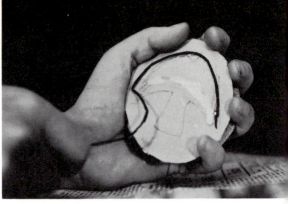

Mix the polymer color with curing agent and allow to set. A longer setting time will give you a thicker easier-to-control flow. The directions on the bottle call for a 5-minute wait for colors to set. I suggest you wait 20 to 30 minutes. Also add a touch of Boss Gloss thickening powder which is designed to keep the enamel from running on vertical surfaces such as rounded stones. When working on flat slate this would not be necessary.

While the enamel is hardening sketch your design on the stone and apply glue all around and into this press the cloisonné, in this case a piece of decorative cord. Don't worry if the glue line is not even, since the glue will dry clear or can be wiped off with a rag.

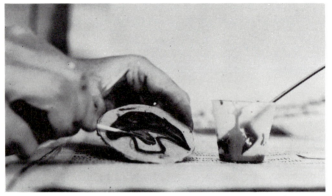

With a toothpick as an applicator, fill the thickened enamel into the design.

Enameled mushrooms. Red caps, white dots, green cord, against a pale beige stone.

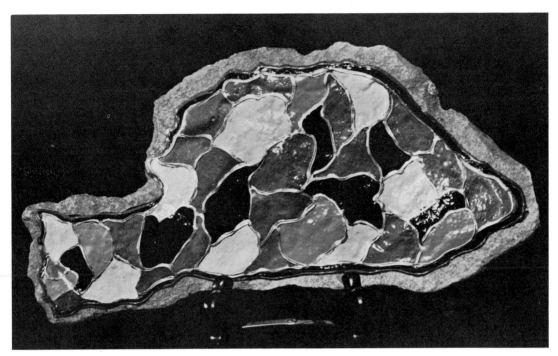

Like most stone artists, Walter Vogel lets the shape of his stone backgrounds help shape his design. In this case, a turtlelike stone inspired this elegant cloisonné enamel. The artist had such a sure and steady hand that even his cloisons were made with thin strips of enamel. He used gold to give an elegant outline to the blues, greens, and black of the design.

If you're timid about doing your enamel freehand, paint in the general background, and then cut out the more intricate design from a small decoupage print. Paste this in place and apply the enamel color on top of it. The paper will be completely covered by the raised enamel. In this slate enamel, the yellow bodies of the chickens were filled in first, and when the yellow enamel hardened, dabs of red for the ruff and black for the eyes were superimposed. The sun is also enameled.

Printing on Stones

Whenever a repeat of a design is used, printing is a fast and handy way to apply it. I experimented with all sorts of printers and found the hard printers such as wood and buttons did not print well on hard stone. The best printers in terms of applying even prints on stone were those cut from potatoes and carrots. I like the carrot best since it is small and can thus get around stone curves and crevices more easily than the larger potato cuts. Printing inks or water-thinned acrylics work well. Rubber stamp ink works very well too. This comes with its own little applicator brush. When printing an allover design in different colors, make a printer for each color.

Slice carrot in half at the widest point and cut a design in the surface by removing parts with a knife. The raised areas will print.

Brush ink onto the printer with a brush.

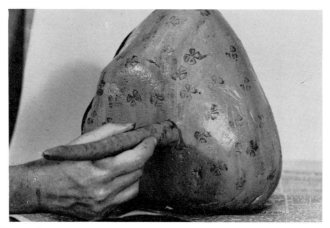

Press the carrot printer over the stone at desired intervals. (See color section for full view of this stone.)

Etched Slate

Etching a design into slate is a noisy business, but it's simple and fun to do. By using odd-shaped pieces of slate (these can be found lying around hillsides and gardens, or had for the asking from masonry suppliers), you can let your background help you to determine the type of etching you want to do.

PAINTING ALTERNATIVES 31

You will want enough details in your etching to give sufficient depth. Don't plan anything too fussy though. If you decide to do a lot of slate etching you may want to invest in a drill with a special fine drilling attachment, such as a Dremel Moto Tool. However, an ordinary electric engraving pen used to mark personal possessions will serve too.

Outline your design with chalk, then groove out with electric engraving pen. Keep a bowl of water and a sponge handy to keep the surface wet. This will make the pen dig in better and also keep dust from flying around.

When your design is etched, wash and dry the slate and fill the grooves with ink. Silver or red ink looks very handsome. You can also rub in a metallic wax such as Rub 'N Buff with a toothpick.

Female head etched on irregular slate. Red ink emphasizes the grooves.

Folk art designs work out very well as slate etchings.

3

USEFUL STONES

SOMETHING BEAUTIFUL REALLY DOESN'T HAVE TO SERVE A PURPOSE. IT CAN JUST *be*. Of course, when something lovely also serves a genuine use, it's a special bonus. The stones in this chapter all have one thing in common: they serve as decorations, but in the process also fulfill a task. It may be to hold open a door or the pages of a book, to tell time, or to serve as a piece of furniture.

This sun-god etched on red slate was glued into the natural ridge found in a piece of weathered wood. A wooden clothespin was cemented to the wood, turning this into a handy holder for notes or outgoing letters.

Doorstops

Large heavy rocks with lots of texture make ideal doorstops or front porch markers. The biggest problem with some of these stones is to gather the strength to lift them up on your worktable.

Bus. In the lower Manhattan area where artist Barton Benes lives there are few rocks or stones to be found, except for large cobblestones. These angular stones seem to suit the artist's interest in American road life. (Gary Wright, photograph)

The almost grotesque shape of this enormous river rock seemed to demand a humorous touch. The colors are bright blue, yellow, and white. For the other side of this droll creature see the color section. (Mike Sommer, artist)

Portrait. (Harriette Trifon, artist)

Jungle animals like this lion and giraffe would make good guards for any door. (Charles Daugherty, Don Coppola, artists)

Slate Bookshelf with Pebble-Covered Pencil or Flower Holders

You will need two empty soup cans, a large slab of slate, and lots of little pebbles. The easiest way to adhere pebbles to cans is to make some bread dough which is quick and inexpensive household clay. To make the dough, remove the crusts from white bread and crumble it into small bits. Add a heaping teaspoonful of white glue to every three slices of bread, plus a few drops of detergent or glycerine. Knead this mixture together until it no longer sticks to your hands. (A three-slice formula should cover two small orange juice cans. If you make a larger formula, wrap up the leftovers in a plastic bag and store in your refrigerator.)

To cover the pencil-holder cans, coat each one with white glue. Roll out the dough as you would for cookies and roll the glue-covered can into the dough.

Now brush the dough-covered cans with glue, spread pebbles on a piece of waxed paper, and roll the cans into the pebbles. Let the cans dry on their sides on waxed paper. The dough will dry hard overnight and the pebbles will be firmly adhered. You could apply the pebbles directly to the cans with cement but I find the bread dough base easier and like the fullness it adds to the shape of the cans.

When the pebble-covered cans are dry, cement them to the end of a slate bookshelf.

Bookmarks

Small stones can serve as attractive bookmarks. Charles Daugherty and Don Coppola mounted theirs on hand-tooled leather (*left*). Carol Lynn Rosenthal painted a blue eye on a black stone and glued this to a circle of blue suede, which in turn was mounted on a black suede strap (*right*). Bugs, butterflies, mushrooms, printed or written words, names, inscriptions, decoupage prints, or photographs could all make appropriate motifs. Ordinary colored strings, skinny thongs, or bolo cords could be used as less elaborate straps.

Bookends

Plexiglass sheets are easy to bend with a simple heating tool available in all stores selling plexiglass supplies (see Sources of Supplies). Apply this heating rod at the spot where you want your bookend to bend and hold in place long enough for the plexiglass to give and bend. That's all you have to do. Mount a decorated stone either with double-sided tape if you plan to switch stones around, or with clear cement. This cute little mouse on sodalite stone is by Charles Le Norrey.

This bookend is really a collaborative effort. When I added this painted head by Susan Vaeth to my collection, I wanted to be able to admire the mustachioed fellow from all angles since it is completely three-dimensional. An inexpensive wooden bookend seemed to be a perfect body. In order not to detract from the head, the suit was painted a conservative navy with a light blue shirt. A red and white striped tie added a dash of color.

Slate Clock

A highly original clock can be created quite simply by drilling a hole into the center of a 6-inch slate square, and then inserting a clock movement.

To drill the hole into slate you will need a masonry bit attached to a ¼-inch drill. Your slate should not be thicker than ¼ inch or you will have difficulty finding a clock with a shank deep enough to fit through the hole.

There are many ways you can decorate slate clocks. Numbers, the signs of the zodiac, photographs or drawings of friends or family members, flowers, etc., could either be painted or made with decoupage. Numbers would be very effective if etched in (see etching in Chapter 2).

Instead of slate you might even use a piece of thin marble, also available from stone masonry suppliers. One-fourth-inch marble is not usually available in the handy sizes of slate but most suppliers will cut it to size for a nominal charge.

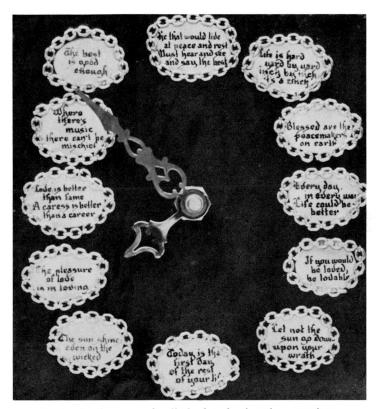

Instead of numerals, little hand-printed quotations were glued to this greenish slate clock. A chain patterned gold braid paper, available in any hobby shop selling decoupage supplies, was glued in place as a border. The clock was not inserted until the designs were coated with ten coats of decoupage finish and rubbed down with wet and dry sandpaper, fine steel wool, and a finish of paste wax. (See decoupage in Painting Alternatives, Chapter 2.)

Tissue Collage Slate Table

A large piece of slate can make a handsome cocktail or side table. Several pieces can be cemented into a frame if you want a larger table. The frame consists of four strips of 1¼-inch wood nailed to a piece of plywood which has been cut to fit the size of the slate. The illustrated side table is 11 inches square. Legs of any height are available at lumberyards.

A tabletop can be painted, etched, trimmed with decoupage, or left plain. The illustrated table was done with a collage of cut tissue paper. The design was based on some Chinese Tanagram puzzles. These puzzles consist of seven basic shapes which can be combined to make an enormous variety of figures. In making the table, red tissue paper was actually cut into the seven basic shapes. The pieces were then glued down to form the figure. When handling colored tissue, brush it with acrylic medium which is a pasting and a glazing agent. Apply the wet tissue very carefully to the background to avoid bleeding edges. The color of the slate (green was used in the illustration) will shimmer through the tissue. Acrylic medium is brushed on several times for a protective finish and to build up the texture of slate and tissue.

Tissue collage slate table by the author.

4

STONE ASSEMBLAGES

Assemblage is actually an extension of collage. Both forms of art involve assembling, arranging, and gluing various materials to a surface. Collage is done primarily with flat materials; assemblage utilizes a greater variety of materials, many of them three-dimensional or sculptural.

Stones are marvelous assemblage materials. Whether you use painted or unpainted stones, whether you arrange them realistically or abstractly, is up to you. In this chapter you will see examples of stone assemblages which are primarily decorative, as well as examples where artists have used the stones to make serious artistic statements.

Arline Shapiro has long been a beachcomber, using the driftwood, stones, and other things washed ashore to create her commentaries on the human condition. In this piece which she calls *Cruising*, she has drawn ink portraits on a variety of stones and mounted them onto the driftwood which reminded her of a ship. The birds, which are natural stone formations, might indeed perch atop any ship's railing. The artist attaches her stones with a plaster she mixes herself. However, household cement will hold most stones in place firmly and permanently.

More pebble people! These pen-and-ink portraits are a good way to learn to catch facial characteristics. A judicious selection of stones will do all your shading and facial contouring for you. Often, when you look closely at a pebble, you will see distinct markings exactly where eyes, nose, or mouth would go. You can add some color to black ink drawings by introducing red mouths, or colored ink for hair. I particularly like brown ink and at times mix my own deep sepia by mixing transparent brown with opaque black ink. Fine line permanent magic markers are usable too. If you put a fine line brown and/or black marker in your bag, you can do some of your faces as you gather the stones.

An old cigar box is used to house all types of stone faces. To keep this assemblage from being too heavy, the bottom half of the box is filled with packing case Styrofoam. The stones are glued in as top layers. The heads are turned every which way, often crowded in and almost invisible, in keeping with my title: *Boxed-In*.

Dee Weber spent a day combing the beach for pebbles which would suggest the shapes and shades of the many kinds of people revolving around the sun. She chose black burlap and an elegant gold frame to mount her people.

A multimedia assemblage combining stones, packing case Styrofoam, and framed canvas. The faces have beautiful natural contours and shadings to help the artist present her statement. The framed canvas was painted with white gesso. If you decide to try some assemblages using Styrofoam as an integral part of your background but want the foam to be less easily identifiable, try using a blow torch with a very small flame all along the edges. This creates a very soft texture. (*Written on the Wall*. Justine R. Schacter, artist)

A piece of barn siding was stained a rich green. Touches of the green accent the black ink features of all the people *On the Wall*. (Arline Shapiro, artist; collection of Mrs. Ruth Kallman)

Shadow Boxes

Stones embedded into Styrofoam and framed in simple wood frames make unique assemblages. A group of small shadow boxes makes an interesting wall grouping.

Use 1" Styrofoam to embed the rock. The Styrofoam can be cut with an ordinary kitchen knife. Cut the block at least an inch larger all around than the stone or stones you plan to embed. Use a spoon to gouge out enough of the Styrofoam so that the stone will fit in and be level with the edges of the block. The foam may be left white or green (the colors in which it is available) or sprayed with spray paint.

Glue the stone (painting or ink drawing should by made before embedment) into the gouged-out space, using either white glue or Duco cement.

The finished shadow box is framed by simply nailing or gluing together four pieces of ¼" wood which can be stained or painted. Shown here *Peasant with Child* and *Eskimo Child* by Justine R. Schacter.

Here are some ideas for assemblages especially good for the beginning artist to try:

Abstract Collage. Ordinary pebbles found on the sidewalk of a suburban street are painted hot pink, with just a few lines of darker shading, almost like a lollipop. Smaller, more pointed stones were painted green for leaves. Colored paper is cut into the shape of a vase and mounted on a matching cutout of cardboard. A pressed wood plaque (any inexpensive backing would do) is covered with brown burlap. A small piece of pink burlap is raveled and glued down to serve as a place mat for the vase. When vase and pebbles are glued in place some final touches are added: a gold paper braid is glued around the vase, and some tiny playing cards are scattered on the place mat. The finished plaque is protected with several coats of plastic spray.

Grape Still Life. Rounded pebbles ranging from tiny round stones to larger (approximately 1″) oval ones are arranged on a wooden plaque to form a cluster of white grapes. Yellow stones are also very attractive and easy to find. If you look a bit harder you can also find various shades of pink pebbles which are truly "delicious." (See color section.) For your grape leaves, use any rough-textured stones. The grape leaves shown here are bits of scrap soapstone. This is a soft carving stone which usually has a greenish tint and can be cut with a knife.

To assemble the grape clusters, place the largest pebbles near the top and taper down to a point with the smallest pebbles. Glue down the basic cluster with household cement. The three-dimensional effect is achieved by gluing more pebbles on top of the base. The upper part of the cluster should have three or four layers of stones. The thicker the grape cluster, the more attractive the plaque. After the cement has set, spray the grapes with several coats of clear plastic spray. For a very elegant and more stylized look you might try spraying the white grapes with a coat of pearl finish.

Slab Collage. This ballet dancer is made up of broken bits of beautiful green and pink conglomerate stones found at a flea market. The seller had a tray of these tucked at the very edge of his exhibit of more "collectible" stones. By shuffling the stones around, all sort of shapes began to emerge. The two pieces which make up the ballerina's skirt determined the overall shape.

The background is an irregular piece of red slate. Household cement was used as an adhesive.

Decoupage Stone Collage. These small children were cut from a children's book by Kate Greenaway. Two beige-toned pebbles were used to create a mushroom tree for the children to lean against. The mushroom stem was glued down flat against the weathered wood background. The mushroom cap was glued on top of the stem to create height and shadow. The sun is cut yellow paper mounted on cardboard for height. Since decoupage gluing is best done with white glue this was used as an adhesive for everything. The finished plaque was brushed with three coats of acrylic gloss medium, which gives a textured finish and blends well with the weathered wood.

Cecile Fine collected hundreds upon hundreds of flat smooth pebbles during a summer at Napeague Bay on Long Island. She grouped her pebbles according to their predominant shape and drew her design inspiration from such natural sources as a shadow falling through leaves, or a haiku poem. To exploit the natural colors of her stones, she worked on a neutral ground, unprimed duck, stretched on standard canvas stretchers. The artist's designs are abstract, but you could use her technique for realistic assemblages and collages too. For variety of texture, sand, wire, stretched cheesecloth, and an occasional spray of colored paint can be used. The pebbles used here are absolutely flat and very light and could be adhered to the background with white glue or acrylic medium. For heavier rounder pebbles a large board of weathered or stained wood and a heavy household cement are recommended.

Cinnamon. Cecile Fine.

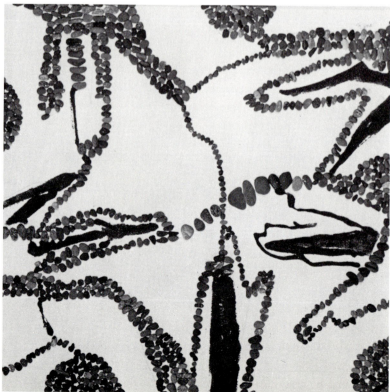

The Round. Cecile Fine. (From the collection of Isidore and Ethel Cytron)

Marion McChesney calls her combinations of variously shaded and shaped stones Kaleidoscopes. She embeds her designs in an interesting background of glue, water, and sand which dries to a rich, hard, and very durable finish.

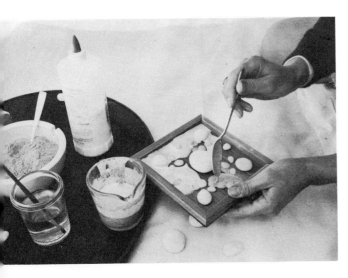

Stones are glued to a framed wooden background. A mixture of ½ Elmer's Glue, ½ water and sand is poured all around the design. The mixture should be in a fairly liquid state. The glue will dry clear, leaving the sand somewhat darker, with a hard sheen.

Since the mixture is water soluble, a brush can be dipped in water and used to clean off the stones.

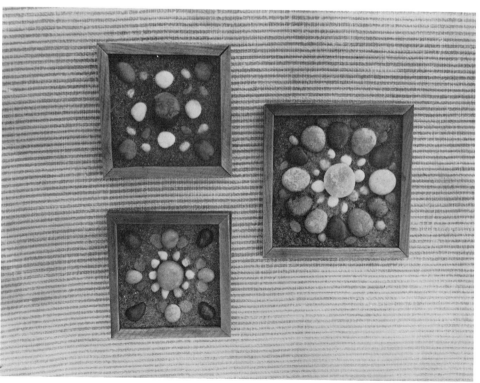

Three stone Kaleidoscopes set in a background of glue-water-sand. The design gains its interest from the various shades of the stones.

5

SCULPTURE

To some sculptors who carve in stone and marble, or cast large pieces, pebbles and rocks serve as inspirational springboards. Jacques Lipchitz attributes many of his ideas for sculptural form to chance observations of natural forms such as rocks. Even as a very young artist, Henry Moore collected pebbles and flints on the beaches of Kent, Norfolk, and Dorset counties in England. These natural forms served as inspiration and some of these original "models" for his large and famous pieces are still in his studio.

You don't have to go into carving and chiseling or casting of bronzes to be a stone sculptor. You can create sculptures by building stones into three-dimensional forms. No welding tools are needed, just good working adhesives such as epoxy or glue. Your sculptures can be made from natural, unpainted stones, or stones with painted details. The painted sculptures tend to be decorative, and often humorous. Unpainted sculptures offer more of an opportunity to make a statement and demand the direct involvement of the viewer.

Jean Kawecki has developed a most unusual and beautiful technique in her combination of stone and copper. She collects stones wherever she goes but finds that Sussex County, New Jersey, particularly the Franklin Mineral Dump, yields the most interesting specimens. Looking at her sculptures it is often hard to believe that the stones have not been chiseled or carved.

The copper used for heads and arms and other details is simply worked with snips, pliers, hammer, and a T square. To give the copper a soft antique look that blends in with the earth-toned rocks she favors, the artist oxidizes it with liver of sulphur (sulfurated potash) which is available in most art stores. If the oxidation needs some highlights, a little kitchen cleanser such as Ajax or Comet will work as well as anything else.

To join the copper to the stone an epoxy known as PC 7 (see Sources of Supplies) is used. This is a paste form epoxy which forms an extremely strong bond, stronger in fact than the stone. At times this epoxy paste is used for visual effects—to build up a stone or to give additional texture— as well as to give strength and stability. Once the epoxy is set it can be tinted to blend into the stone so that the average eye cannot distinguish between stone and adhesive. Any good exterior latex paint can be used. It is possible to achieve all the necessary tones with a small range of colors: black, white, brown, green, or yellow.

The stones are set into a walnut base which is gouged out so that the stone balances itself in the required position. If one finds the center of gravity it is possible to set a very large stone on a very small point and then hold it in position with the epoxy paste.

Again, you might want to try something small first, such as the bird held in the hand of this beautiful figure. Note the natural feminine contours of the stone. (*Release* by Jean Kawecki, artist; collection of Trudy and Sol Schwartz)

Until you get the feel of handling the copper which combines so handsomely with these very rough stones, you might want to try doing some very small pieces such as the tiny chicks in this barnyard grouping. Only tiny beaks of copper are needed. If you look closely at the rooster's ruff and tail you will see that everything is cut from one piece of copper which is draped around the stone. (*Life with Father* by Jean Kawecki, artist)

The neck of the mother in this beautiful family group is built up with extra epoxy which is colored to match the body stone. (*Family Group* by Jean Kawecki, artist; collection of author)

More Natural Stone Sculptures

In the previous pages we saw stone sculptures welded together with an epoxy bond. These smaller sculptures, also made up only of natural stones, were glued together with strong white glue. The glue is poured in very freely, and when the piece has set overnight, another layer of glue is poured in for a double set. The glue dries clear. The pieces should lie on their sides, lean against other stones, or be taped together with masking tape while the glue is setting (see gluing demonstration for Stone Whimsies in following pages). For very lightweight stones you may prefer to use a quick-setting epoxy such as 5-Minute Epoxy which literally sets up in the stated time.

A wood base is gouged out with a sharp pocket knife so that the sculpture can be solidly mounted with good balance. White glue is poured into the hole and when the stone has set and hardened, another small cementing layer of glue is poured around the edges. This will dry clear.

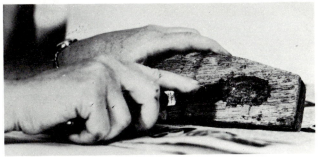

When you collect stones for natural sculptures, try to find different shapes which have matching grains and lines. These two stones were obviously made for each other. (*Pregnant Woman* by Mike Sommer)

When you start looking for odd-shaped stones, you will find quite a lot with large protrusions which seem to just naturally suggest funny noses (see painted stones in color section and bookends in Chapter 3). This head is white, the stone base and hat are brown. (*Le Grand Charles* by Mike Sommer)

Two thin flat stones are glued together, with the head at a bent angle. A brown stone is glued in place on each side of the figure to suggest a bag or bucket into which the shell collector can put her finds. The mica stone base is covered with small shells from the Florida beaches.

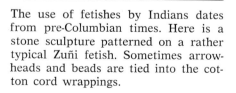

The use of fetishes by Indians dates from pre-Columbian times. Here is a stone sculpture patterned on a rather typical Zuñi fetish. Sometimes arrowheads and beads are tied into the cotton cord wrappings.

Conversation with Death. Like Jean Kawecki, Mike Sommer does not look for pretty stones. Here conglomerates (pebbles which get cemented in with sand) mounted on dull brown stones and a light stone base are used to express an abstract theme.

Holocaust. Mike Sommer. This sculpture was built up in several stages. The odd-shaped stones seemed to dictate their own path.

Stone Whimsies

To create these whimsical creatures, all you need is a sense of humor. Each one is made up of four base stones easily found almost anywhere. While you can paint in detailed features and clothing, these little characters are cutest when left seminude, with just bits of wire, shell, clothing, and a few dabs with a magic marker to suggest details. It is when picking out the accessories and mountings that the real fun begins: fingers from old gloves can be used as ski hats; spool wire can be glued on as goggles; shells can be used as hats, skirts, aprons; string dipped into glue as hair. Popsicle sticks can be used as skis, seesaws, and spears; large stones can be put together to serve as horses and strange animals on which the whimsical riders sit.

If you're having an informal party, glue together some basic whimsies, provide your guests with a box of accessory materials and have a "happening." Your guests will do impressions of each other, famous people, and perhaps some infamous ones. (See color section for whimsical skier.)

Sometimes the base stone will suggest the whimsy, as in this case: A broken stone seemed a perfect whale for a whimsical Jonah. The beard is white cotton, the oar a toothpick.

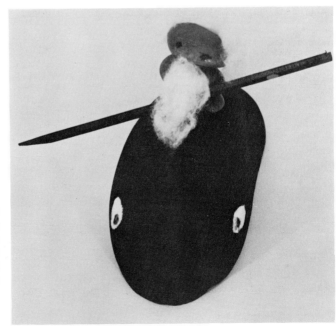

Whimsical Nudenik has hair made from black cotton thread dipped in glue, glasses from gold spool wire, and a tiny bouquet of dried flowers held in place by a bit of shell. The fisherman wears a shell hat and nothing else. His oars are toothpicks and his boat is made from two long shells.

Four basic pebbles used to make stone whimsy figures. These may vary in size.

The two large stones are glued together to make the head and body, the two small ones as feet. White glue is used and a strip of masking tape is wrapped around the whimsy while the glue sets.

Hobby paint can be used to paint the whimsy's body. Large stones can be glued together as horses for the whimsies to sit on. Spool wires, shells, magic markers, coffee stirrers and toothpicks all serve as accessories to dress up the whimsy.

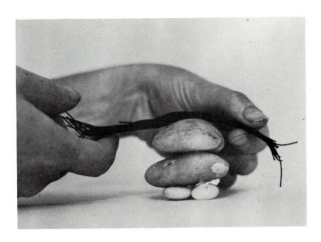

Black thread dipped in glue to stiffen it makes a fine whimsical hairdo.

Stones Embedded in Shaped Plexiglass Sheets

Every day more and more artists and craftsmen are discovering the versatility of plexiglass. Here Jerry Philips demonstrates how a painted stone can be combined with cut and shaped plexiglass to create a very modern and unsual sculpture. Like many rock artists he seems fascinated with the whale, which of course leads to the combination of Jonah and the whale. Undoubtedly this interest in the whale is a combination of the near extinction of the species and the whale shape inherent in many stones.

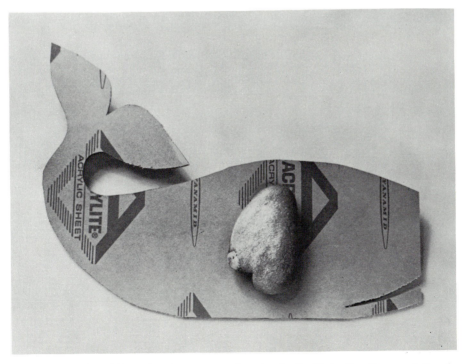

Select a pebble with a simple contour that lends itself to the figure of Jonah. Using the stone as a guide for size, draw the outline of the whale on the protective paper covering a ⅛" thick piece of acrylic plastic sheet. Cut out the whale shape with a coping saw or jigsaw.

Draw the outline of the pebble on a piece of cardboard and cut a hole along this line. Adjust the shape with the pebble until the fit is perfect. The cardboard then becomes a template for the Jonah hole in the plastic sheet. Transfer the outline to the "stomach" of the whale.

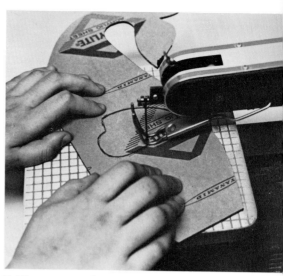
Drill a starter hole within the shape of Jonah and pass the blade through the hole, permitting the saw to work "from the inside." Cut out the Jonah shape with a coping saw or jigsaw.

Refine the Jonah hole and the outer edges of the whale with sandpaper. Power drill emery wheel points can be used to refine the hole, as shown. Polish the outer edges with a muslin wheel dressed with buffing compound. Do not polish the hole edges.

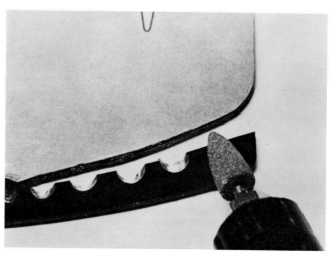
Peel off the protective paper covering the lower jaw and grind away the spaces between the whale's teeth with a file, sandpaper, or emery wheel point. Polish the now toothy jaw very carefully since the slim plastic piece can easily snap off.

Remove the rest of the protective paper and heat the tail section by holding it several inches above a low flame. Be careful not to allow bubbles to form or to have the plastic ignite. When the plastic is soft and floppy, bend the tail to the desired angle and hold in place until the plastic hardens.

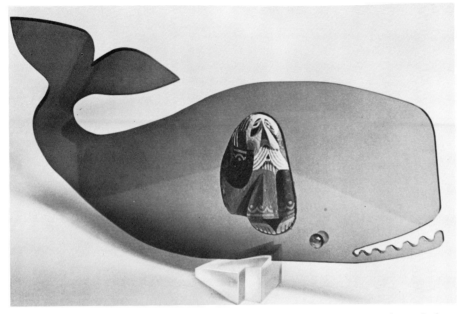

Paint Jonah on the stone. Coat the painted stone with lacquer and set it into hole, using acrylic medium as cement. Allow several hours for drying. Finish off the whale with small acrylic spheres as eyes (cement to the acrylic sheet with methylene chloride or other suitable solvent) and fit the whole thing into a solid acrylic plastic base.

(All photographs for this project by the artist)

If the plexiglass and stone embedment technique is not your thing, keep searching for stones which can just *be* whales—like this handsome fellow discovered at the Bay of Fundy in New Brunswick by William Gorman. The broken section of the stone was a "natural" to hold a tiny Jonah pebble with red hair and a beard. The whale itself called for a very minimum of painting. (Collection of Mr. and Mrs. Carmen Dellapietro)

SCULPTURE

More Sculpture Ideas

At left, *Teddy Bear in a Flower Garden* by Cindy Cohen. Lots of tiny pebbles were glued to a larger stone, painted grass green with dabs of color to suggest flowers. The Teddy bear, consisting of nine pebbles, is painted brown with a white belly and pink ears. At right, a fisherman, complete with stone fish by Arden J. Newsome. The fisherman is made from three irregular stones, one for the body, one for the head, and a gravel stone for the arm. The grasses, NO FISHING sign, and base are also pebbles.

Butterflies lend themselves particularly well to simple sculptural detail. Three stones are glued to the center for a built-up body.

Here is the finished butterfly, painted in brilliant colors against a black background. (Charles Daugherty and Don Coppola, artists)

Ducks are another popular type of animal sculpture. These three are painted in bright blues and oranges. (Carol Lynn Rosenthal, artist)

The muff in this sculpture is a natural formation. The head is a separate stone. Learn to turn stones in every direction to see which way they sit, to capture whatever is suggested and to determine what, if anything, is needed to add in the way of painted detail. (Harriette Trifon, artist)

Jeanie Arnel gives new interest to a wire sculpture with the addition of stones. To make a wire construction you need 16- and 20-gauge wire, wire clippers, and thin-nosed pliers, all available in hardware stores. The stones are slipped into the wire after the sculpture is complete. They can be secured with a bit of household cement. The wire can be sprayed with black paint. This should be done before the stones are inserted.

Tell a Story with Your Stone Sculptures

If you find yourself short of ideas for stone sculptures think of a song, a poem, or a nursery rhyme. Here's the tale of the old woman in the shoe, twice told from rather different points of view.

Jan Gary searched a long time for a rock which would lend itself to a large shoe painting. She constructed a base, roof gable, and chimney from wood. Children are painted all around the shoe. The old lady, a separate stone, sits in one corner of the yard, head in hands, for she really *doesn't* know what to do.

My own Old Woman sculpture evolved from an old wooden shoe bought at a junk shop. Styrofoam is stuffed into the bottom of the shoe and the old woman and her children are glued on top of this. A large, yellowish rock was used for the old woman. The children's heads are variously shaped and skin toned. The faces are drawn with a fine line sepia marker. There are *so* many children that they spill over the edges of the shoe—one child even clings to the back of the sad old woman's head. Since my basic purpose was to make the old nursery rhyme relevant to our present-day world my title is *Population Explosion*.

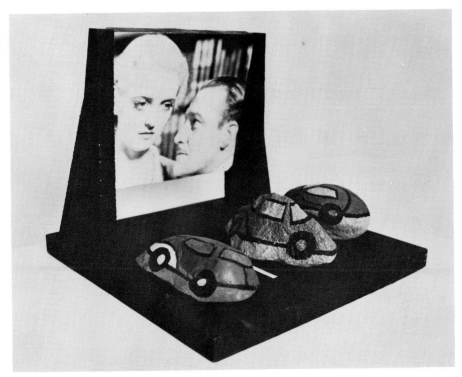

Barton Benes's fascination with America on the move led him to build a marvelous environment for his stone cars. This drive-in movie is quite simply constructed from pieces of wood which were painted black. You could superimpose your own favorite movie on the screen.

Arline Shapiro loves to combine her finds from nature. At left, a natural dancing figure of driftwood with an ink drawn stone head. At right, another driftwood and stone figure. The flowers on both sculptures are stones cemented to wire. (*Dancer*, collection of Mr. and Mrs. Robert Black; *Poet*, collection of Mr. and Mrs. Marshall Luskoff)

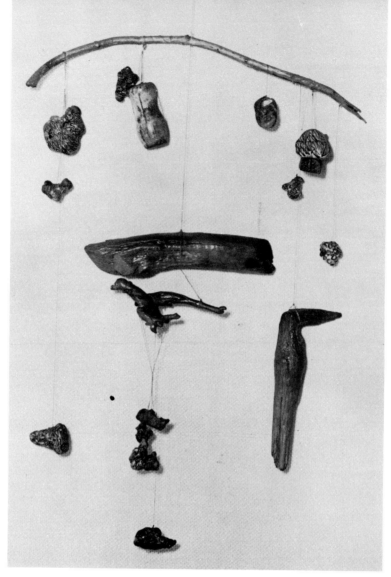

A charming mobile can be made from twigs, driftwood formations, and stones. The stones have only the most minimal inked detail. (Arline Shapiro, artist)

Playing with Stones—a Stone Chess Set

Chess pieces have been a challenge to many sculptors. A chess set made with stones is unique. William Gorman's chess set with its painted beach pebble heads and carved wooden bases might seem like an enormous undertaking at first glance. However, those carved bodies are merely a clever compilation of hardware and lumberyard materials.

The materials used are wooden shade roller dowels, decorative spindles, ⅛" dowels for spears, decorative upholstery tacks, and shade roller ends for shields. The artist's tools are quite simple: penknives, small woodcut tools of Japanese designs, small files, a coping saw, sandpaper, and white glue.

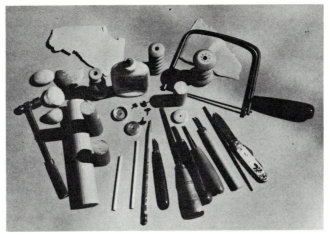

Materials for making carved body and stone head chess set.

Main pieces of chess set. (William Gorman, artist)

The bodies are roughly cut out of dowels (except where decorative spindles are used) which are shaped very loosely with a penknife and carved with the woodcut tools, files, and sandpaper. When the body is completed it is painted with acrylics and the painted stone head is glued in place. The spears and shields are glued and put into place and the whole mounted on small pedestals.

Other materials which could be used for spears might be wooden matchsticks for small figures, or wooden chopsticks for larger ones. By using only decorative spindles, drawer pulls, wooden spools, or large wooden beads glued on top of each other, you can eliminate carving altogether.

Other chess set ideas: Make heads and bodies for your chessmen out of stone. Use tiny pebbles glued together for pawns, larger pebbles for other pieces. Mount all on equally sized wooden blocks and distinguish with different colored paints or inks. You could also cut pieces of packing case Styrofoam into chess bodies, paint them with acrylics, and mount stone heads on top of each. Different sized Styrofoam cones can be cut into chess pieces with stone heads too (see Stone Head Place Card Holder, Chapter 8).

Soapstone Carving

No discussion of stone sculpture can really be considered complete without a word about carving. All the techniques previously shown involved building stone upon stone.

Most amateur craftsmen seem intimidated by the thought of carving and chipping away from a large, hard mass. However, if you look at the work done by the Eskimos with soft natural steatite or soapstone, and a simple hand-fashioned knife, you will realize that you need neither complicated carving tools nor very hard stones to create beautiful work.

You might find some natural deposits of soapstone in your area. The Eskimos who don't live on the east coast of Hudson Bay, which has numerous steatite deposits, often travel long distances by boat for their supplies. They quarry their stone simply by using a larger, harder stone as a sledgehammer and shattering pieces from the main body of the rock.

You can buy soapstone very inexpensively from any sculpture supply house.

While you can carve with a sharp knife, you will probably want to add a steel rasp to your supplies, to help you refine your contours; also a small diamond needle to etch in details. The Eskimos use steel needles for this purpose.

To give a finish to your stone you can again follow the technique of the Eskimos, using a rough stone and perhaps sand. An oil sealer will protect and darken the stone. The Eskimos submerge their carvings in seal oil for two days. Stone dust, rottenstone, and wet and dry sandpaper can be used for a final hand-polishing and smoothing. These materials are available in hardware and hobby stores.

Philapushee, Grise Fiord artist, carving steatite with simple knife. (Photograph courtesy Department of Indian Affairs and Northern Development, Government of Canada)

Innuk, a Frobisher Bay artist, etching detail into soapstone. (Photograph courtesy Department of Indian Affairs and Northern Development, Government of Canada)

Walrus carving by Tguplait of Repulse Bay (Photograph courtesy Information Canada, Photothèque)

6

MOSAICS

Mosaics are designs made of small pieces of tesserae. Pebble mosaics are the oldest form of the technique. The pebbles in the mosaics in Pella, Greece, date back to 300 B.C. The naturally tinted pebbles were roughly matched and embedded in cement which was allowed to show between the stones. The subjects of these mosaics were adolescent figures, lion and stag hunts, and borders with wreaths of plants. Originally used as palace floors, these lovely mosaics, many of which have only been excavated in recent years, have been set upright as wall mosaics.

In the following pages you will see examples of modern mosaics embedded in plaster, in the manner of these early Greek works, as well as mosaic embedments in such definitely twentieth-century materials as Styrofoam.

Pebbles can also be glued directly to boards of wood or Masonite and slate. This is probably the simplest method, and to get started in stone mosaic making you might try looking for pieces of slate or wood with shapes which suggest a particular form. You can then work your stones to utilize this basic background shape.

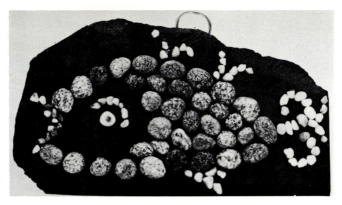

This piece of slate suggested the shape of a fish and a collection of tweedy gray pebbles captures the texture of the fish skin. Tiny white pebbles were used for color contrast and the fish fins. The only painted touch is the pupil of the eye. Household cement is used to adhere the stones to the slate.

Another fish shape, this time a wood die-cut discard. This seemed to call for quite a different sort of design. The plaque is thick and not very graceful looking. It brought to mind all the human fish tossed about in the sea of life—helter-skelter, big and little, rarely in perfect grace and symmetry. With this concept it seemed natural to fill in the plaque with a lot of large and little pebble portraits and to call the result, *BIG FISH—little fish*. Note the different colors of the "fish," the angles and planes of the stones, and the irregular placement.

Styrofoam and Stone Mosaics

When working out a large mosaic plaque where an entire surface will be covered with stones, some uniformity in the surface is desirable. This can be achieved if you use only perfectly flat, even pebbles. When stones have different thicknesses, you can embed them in plaster (see following pages). A very easy and flexible method is to use a background of Styrofoam. The pebbles can be pressed into the Styrofoam and glued into this indentation. Flat pebbles will be pressed in very lightly; fatter pebbles will be glued into deeper indentations. To strengthen the foam, brush each side with two coats of acrylic gesso. If you plan to let some of the Styrofoam show, tint the gesso with water-based paint.

After the Styrofoam base has been primed with two coats of gesso on each side, sketch in your design with pencil.

Sort the pebbles and press each one into the Styrofoam to make the desired indentation—flat pebbles and fat pebbles will be level according to the depth of the indentation made for each.

The finished plaque is framed, sprayed with clear plastic spray. (See color section for different colors used.)

Pick up each pebble and apply cement from a tube into the indentation. Press the pebble back in place.

A Styrofoam wreath is used to create a mosaic frame. The centers of the flowers are tiny yellow pebbles, the leaves are pieces of gravel and the spaces in between are filled in with round white pebbles.

Cement and Rock Mosaics

Kay Weiner demonstrates how to embed a rock and pebble design into a box frame container filled with cement. (All photographs by Scott Aruta).

Assemble all materials: Box frame constructed from plywood (the frame pictured is 2" deep and securely fastened to a ¾" plywood base), colored stones, mixing pail, cement shovel, picture wire, water base paint if color is desired for cement, Sakrete (a plaster premix of sand and cement; 20 lbs. is sufficient for approximately 3 square feet), working gloves.

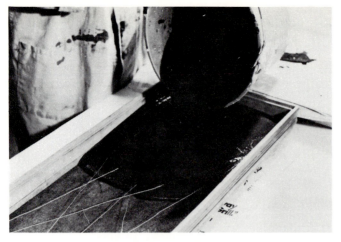

Attach and crisscross several strands of picture wire inside base of frame with screw eyes or nails. This will help to secure the cement in frame once it is hardened. Mix the Sakrete with water according to directions and pour into the frame until it is ½ to 1" thick.

Arrange the rocks gently in the soft cement.

Brass lead or rope strips can be incorporated into the design for more definite division of areas. The cement will begin to harden within half an hour. As the moisture rises to the surface, soak it up with paper towels. The project will be dry within 24 hours.

A finished cement and rock mosaic. The frame can be painted or lacquered. The completed mosaic design should be coated with clear lacquer. It can be hung indoors or out. With the addition of a base and a glass top, it could be turned into a unique table.

Fascinating rock and cement mosaics made from stones found along Israel's coast. Odd-shaped bits of clay blend in well with the many large and odd-shaped stones which make up the center design. Flat square tessera stones are worked in between the large ones. The plaster was tinted pink. A wood frame to hold the cement was built on top of a plywood plaque. (Motke Blum, artist)

Another rock and cement mosaic by Israeli artist Motke Blum.

7

JEWELRY

JEWELRY MADE FROM FOUND STONES MAY NOT REQUIRE AN INSURANCE FLOATER from Lloyd's of London, but it is guaranteed to be a compliment catcher wherever it's worn. The types of jewelry you can make can only be touched upon here. All the painting and painting alternative techniques described in Chapters 1 and 2 can be used for your stone jewelry. Unusually shaped or colored stones can be simply mounted. Some stones can even be leaded, like stained glass. As you try out some of the projects described, your own ideas will take shape and develop.

In order to make your stones wearable, you need a variety of mechanical fittings or findings. Many inexpensive and useful findings with either gold or rhodium finishes are available from crafts or jewelry suppliers (see Sources of Supplies).

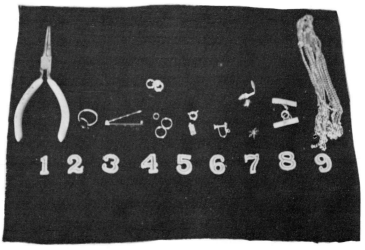

Shown here are some of the materials and findings needed to turn your stones into pendants, necklaces, or rings: 1. A fine-nosed plier is an important tool for opening and closing jump rings and cutting chains. 2. Adjustable rings with flat tops. 3. Pinbacks come in various lengths; a large pinback, placed ⅓ from the top, makes for a pin that "sits" right. 4. Jump rings are important connectors and come in many sizes. 5. Necklace closings; at bottom a type of closing where a thin piece pushes inside a little box; at top a lock which requires a jump ring as a partner. 6. Earring findings. 7. Bellcaps open up to fit around the top of a stone, thus turning it into a pendant. They come in different sizes; the type shown at bottom requires a jump ring for the chain, the other kind has its own loop. For very small stones you could substitute a finding known as an upeye which covers less of the stone. 8. Clasps which fit around ribbons are useful when making chokers. 9. Chains in various patterns, finishes, and widths are most economically bought by the foot. You can then attach your own jump rings, closing, etc. Findings are attached with clear jeweler's cement.

Jewelry

Necklace and Earrings

Beautiful tweed-textured stones found at Rocky Point, Long Island, are attached with a series of bellcaps and jump rings to form an elegant necklace. Two small stones are made into dangling earrings. If you plan to make lots of jewelry you might eventually want to invest in a small stone tumbler which will polish beach stones to a gorgeous luster. However, a few coats of clear plastic spray will do a good job and will not detract from the natural beauty of the stones.

Ideas for Rings

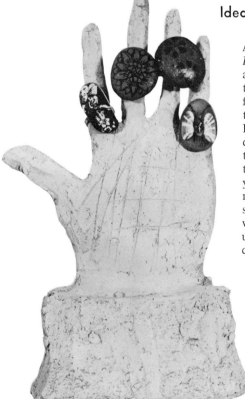

A handful of quick and easy-to-make rings. *From left to right:* Decoupage print against a stone painted black. For small items like this, one of the nicest and easiest protective finishes for your print is to brush it with three coats of clear, undiluted white glue. Fine line magic marker designs can be drawn wherever or whenever you pick up the stone; for hard-edged repeats, try this throwaway stencil idea: hold a doily over your stone and apply color with fine line marker or brush through the holes; two small shells with delicate shadings form the wings of a butterfly, and a skinny stone is used as the body. Fine line marker is used to draw on butterfly antennae.

Close-up details of shell butterfly ring.

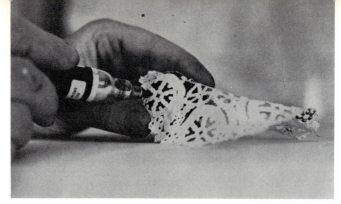

Applying design through throwaway doily stencil.

Rings, Pendants, Bolos, and Key Ring Holders

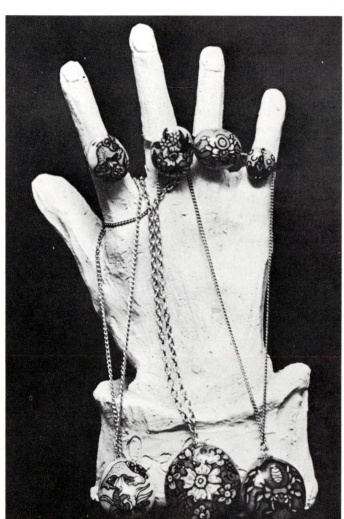

Rings with matching pendants. (Charles Daugherty and Don Coppola, artists)

A variety of pins. *From left to right:* Painted profile (Arden J. Newsome, artist); Painted Americana theme (Susan Vaeth, artist); enameled lizard on stone (Walter Vogel, artist); two pieces of broken agates and a tumbled gemstone are glued together to form a butterfly pin (Elyse Sommer, artist)

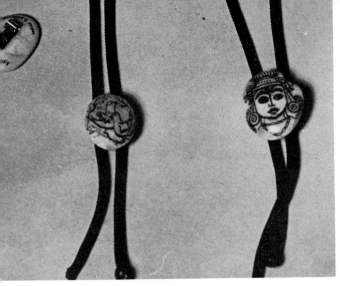
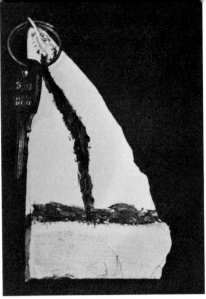

Another way to wear decorated stone is to attach a bolo clasp to the back. It can then be worn around the neck and is suitable for both men and women. Quadruple the length of the rope and you can wear your bolo as an adjustable belt. (Justine R. Schacter, artist)

Odd-shaped pieces of slate make useful and attractive key ring holders. This one had to be a boat for a fisherman friend.

Belt

A belt with a mock stone buckle makes a most unusual fashion buckle. The belt illustrated was made from a 2" wide burlap ribbon (this is sturdy, ravel free, and available in embroidery and knitting stores). The stone "buckle" is cemented to the center of the belt. The actual closing is at the back. Pieces of velcro are glued to either closing end with cement. The stone combines painting with decoupage.

Bracelet

Tic-Tac-Toe Bracelet. The technique for making the belt can be carried through into a fun-and-games bracelet to wear and enjoy during a long trip or for an afternoon at the beach. Cut a 3" wide burlap ribbon (or leather or suede) to fit your wrist. Cement strips of velcro to either end for easy closing. Collect nine gravel stones and paint 4 in one color and 5 in another. Cut velcro into tiny squares to fit the stones and glue one part of the velcro to the back of the stone and the matching part to the bracelet playboard. To play, the stone pieces are lifted off, then pressed back on the board. The illustrated bracelet is in white burlap, with red and blue stones.

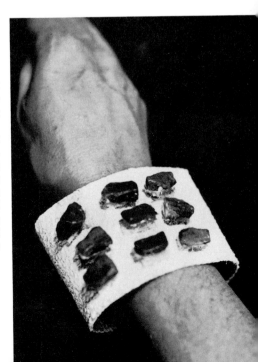

Macramé-Look Pendant

Shade pull rings are attached to one another with gold spool wire. You can also sew them together with invisible thread. Those of you who know how to do macramé can combine your stones with the "real thing." For macramé instructions, see *Macramé Accessories* by Dona Z. Meilach.

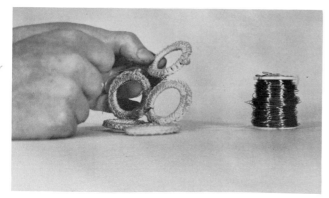

The look of macramé is achieved instantly with the help of cotton cord shade pulls. Decorated stones are glued into the rings which can be arranged in many pendant patterns. The necklace portion is a piece of metal, with the ends bent to interlock.

Leaded Stones

Here's an idea borrowed from the stained glass enthusiasts, to give you a really different piece of jewelry. By wrapping your stones with lead you will be giving them an old, antique effect. This is also a fantastic way of joining stones into a unified whole.

Use stones which are not so thin that they will slip out of the lead wrapping, but not so thick that the leading won't really show. A ¼" depth is ideal.

Supplies for leading stones: $\frac{1}{16}$" U Came lead, flux (this should be brushed on the lead so that the solder will adhere better), solder (60 percent tin and 40 percent lead), and soldering iron. All supplies available from stained glass suppliers and hobby shops. (See Sources of Supplies.) The soldering iron rests on a handmade stand, a block of wood with a triangle carved out.

Wrap lead tightly around the stone and cut off the end with X-Acto knife or single-edged razor blade.

Heat soldering iron and pick up solder with heated iron, then apply to the parts of the lead to be welded together. Any bumps or extra solder can be smoothed down with the flat part of your iron.

From left to right: Four small stones leaded together to create a perky angel. The stones are painted on each side. The hanger is made out of lead. In addition to serving as a pendant, this could be hung as a holiday ornament or become part of a mobile. Three graduated stones. Stained glass experts usually prefer making their hanging hooks out of fine wire but for these chunky pieces, the heavier lead hook seems to fit best. Two stones leaded to make a large pussycat pin. Small pieces of lead are bent and soldered on for the cat's ears. When making leaded jewelry it is visually effective to leave some of the leaded areas open.

Pieces of broken agate are leaded together to make a large mushroom pendant. Since agates are transparent, this could be hung near a window and enjoyed like a piece of stained glass.

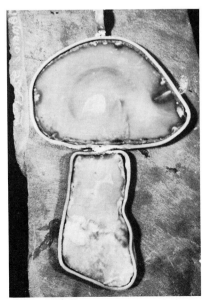

Another way of wrapping stones—an excellent alternative for young craftsmen who should not work with hot soldering irons: pipe cleaners dipped in glue are wrapped around stones.

The pendant at right was also wrapped, this time by stretching a buckskin thong around the edge of the stone which had been covered with white glue. The surface decoration for the center piece is a pressed leaf mounted with white glue and coated with matte medium. Thongs were also used to mount the stones at left which had convenient natural holes, and the middle stone which had a hole drilled through with an emery bit. (Mary Lou Stribling, artist and photograph)

8

HOLIDAYS AND SPECIAL OCCASIONS

It is largely as a result of a need to get away from the mechanized quality of modern life that crafts have flourished so much in recent years. Holidays particularly bring out the urge to give something truly personal. The rock artist has many opportunities for personalized gifts.

Carol Lynn Rosenthal hand-paints family groups on super-sized cards, using painted stone heads for everyone including the family cat. Collage instead of painting could be used for the card, with figures cut and pasted down, and photograph faces of actual people applied by decoupage onto the stone heads.

Three-dimensional Christmas card. (Carol Lynn Rosenthal, artist. See color section)

HOLIDAYS AND SPECIAL OCCASIONS

Simpler, smaller, single-stone cards can be made too. For example: Paint a red heart on a small round stone and send it to your valentine; draw a little angel or a wreath on a stone at Christmastime; a bunny or a small basket of eggs at Easter; draw a little pen and ink portrait of yourself, or the person to whom you are sending the card; fill a cut paper vase with a bouquet of tiny pebbles.

To make your cards combination greetings and gifts, make your stones usable and detachable. For example, glue a small pinback to your decorated stone, then pin it to the card; punch two holes into the card, then pull through a stone on a necklace chain.

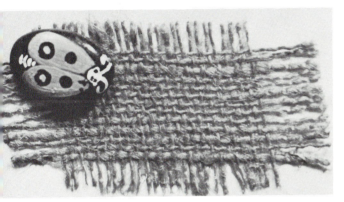

A single stone for a small card that is less elaborate—a tiny stone bug on a piece of raveled burlap. A message inside might read "You're cute as a bug in a rug." (*Stone*, Carol Lynn Rosenthal, artist)

A painted wreath circles a peace dove. This can be hung as a holiday ornament by cementing a beer can hanger to the back. (Charles Daugherty and Don Coppola, artists)

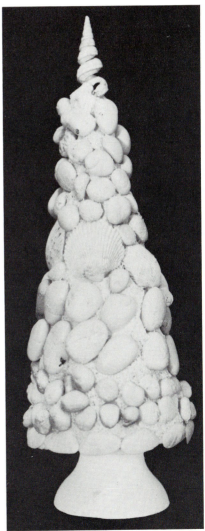

Everyone has room for a miniature tree—like this one made from a Styrofoam cone glued to a drawer pull. Stones and shells are embedded in the tree in a spiraling mosaic pattern. The tree is sprayed with pearl paint for a snowlike finish.

This funny stone just had to be an Easter bunny. Susan Vaeth added a minimum of paint to the naturally bunny-colored stone.

Rocks and Eggs

In recent years the popularity of egg decorating has made this traditionally Easter pastime a year-round hobby. Eggs lend themselves most handsomely to rock crafting. Small rock formations can be used to create a panorama view in an egg which has had a window cut out. Small pebbles can be used to strengthen cut edges, and to add decorative trims and stands.

Goose eggs are ideal for this type of egg decoration since the shells are large and stronger than hen eggs. These are available by mail from various hatcheries and egg craft specialists (see Sources of Supplies). The openings can be cut with a small handsaw, but if you plan to do a lot of eggs, it is suggested that you buy a Dremel Moto tool with a #409 cutting disc which will enable you to make all sorts of special cuts. Some egg craft suppliers will sell the eggs all cut and ready to hinge.

To start, you can achieve charming results with eggs right from your own refrigerator. These can be cut with ordinary manicure scissors or single-edged razor blades.

To cut an egg, mark the opening with a pencil line. With a straight pin punch holes at short intervals all around the opening. Make one hole in the center of the opening.

With manicure scissors (or a single-edged razor) cut slowly from hole to hole. There will be some unevenness to the egg but this will be covered when you decorate.

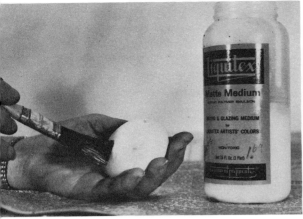

After the egg has been thoroughly washed and allowed to dry, brush it inside and out with several coats of acrylic gloss medium. This will strengthen the shell.

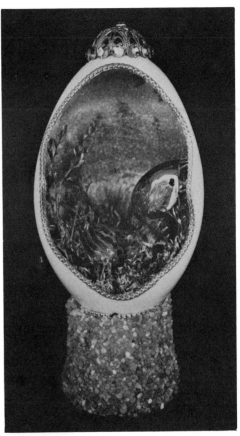

An open goose egg, featuring stones inside and out. The interior background is a paper design glued and glazed with acrylic medium. Stones and weeds are glued to the bottom of the egg. A stone naturally shaped like a duck, and just touched here and there with a bit of paint, nestles on the ground. The egg stand is fashioned from a perfume bottle stopper. Gravel is glued inside this for weight and to the outside to complete the "stony" look. (Julia Hernberg, artist; photograph George Schupka)

The panorama scene in this egg is a natural coral formation to suggest a crèche, set into a colored stone garden. Tiny pebbles are cemented all around the edges of the egg. The back, which is not shown, carries out the religious theme with a pebble cross. (Julia Hernberg, artist; George Schupka, photograph)

A hinged-door goose egg contains a delicate bouquet of white pebble lilies of the valley. If eggs are not your thing, you can nevertheless make some of these easy-to-make, delightful miniature bouquets and use as party decorations. With larger pebbles and heavier bouquets, these might grow into centerpieces. (Julia Hernberg, artist; George Schupka, photograph)

The materials for the lilies of the valley: Neptune of air fern for greenery, tiny white pebbles, air moss, two pieces of limpet shells, varying lengths of fine floral wire wrapped with green thread. The limpet shells are glued together and filled with deer moss as a base. The pebbles are glued to the varying lengths of wire and, together with the greenery, arranged into the base.

HOLIDAYS AND SPECIAL OCCASIONS 83

Pebble Bonsais

A miniature bonsai tree made with pebbles or tiny gemstones is a delightful gift. Use an old cup and saucer or any attractive container for your pot base. Fill this with pebbles and pour white glue throughout the stone base. While the glue is setting, make your tree.

Bonsai arrangement above is made with natural pink beach pebbles. See color section for another bonsai.

Twist two leaf-shaped bellcaps together to make a holder for the pebble leaves.

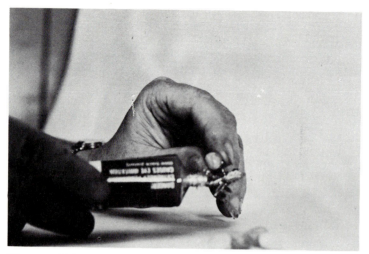

Glue a pebble to each leaf with cement. This step can be saved for later, when the wires are all wrapped and shaped into a tree.

Wrap 30-gauge wire with floral tape. These branches will be twisted to form a bonsai tree.

Stone Head Place Card Holder

Individual place card holders are fun and easy to make. A Styrofoam cone, a round pebble, and some fabric scraps are your main materials.

Cut off a bit from the top of the cone so that the stone can be glued to a wider, sturdier neck.

Drape and glue a piece of fabric around the Styrofoam body. Felt is easy to use since it cuts without raveling. You might drape another piece of dressier fabric over this as a cape. Cut two little hands out of contrasting colored felt, and glue or pin these to either side of the body.

Poke a hole into one of the hands and stick a long thin matchstick through this. Cut a piece of cardboard into the shape of a shield and glue this to the top of the matchstick spear. At party time, write your guest's name on a piece of paper cut to match the shield and attach it with a piece of two-sided Scotch tape. The name tags can thus be changed for every party.

Glue the stone head in place and paint in features and hair.

For a wide-brimmed hat which will hold a bouquet of dried flowers, glue a shell to the stone head. Cut a small square of green floral Styrofoam and stick this to the hat with a piece of floral Stik-It. Arrange the flowers into the Styrofoam.

To make a larger figure which can be used as a table centerpiece, buy the largest Styrofoam cone available, use a larger stone and larger shell and more flowers. Glue the figure to a flat stone or a block of wood so that it will be properly weighted.

Stone place card holder.

9
OWLS AND THE ROCK ARTIST

> A wise old owl sat on an oak,
> The more he saw the less he spoke;
> The less he spoke the more he heard;
> Why aren't we like that wise old bird?
>
> "A Wise Old Owl," Edward Hersey Richards

FROM ANCIENT TIMES OWLS HAVE BEEN SOMETIMES WORSHIPPED AND SOMETIMES feared. They have an almost human look and make almost human sounds. This human quality and the perfect symmetry of the owl's large staring eyes have long fascinated artists. Rock artists are no exception. Sooner or later, every rock artist gets the urge to "do an owl." To give you some ideas for the time when the owl urge grabs you, here are nearly a dozen of my favorite owls.

From left to right: A very straggly fellow, enameled onto slate (Walter Vogel, artist); two black owls with glue and gold bodies perch on a handsome little suede plaque (Carol Lynn Rosenthal, artist); mini owls made of earth-colored flat pebbles, nestling on a pebble branch. The slate plaque is made to stand like an easel with the aid of a rock cemented to the back. (Arden J. Newsome, artist)

Brass lamp parts, wire wheel polishers from a rotary hand tool, lamp parts, washers, artist's pen points, and other hardware and art supply discards make up the fanciful faces of these owls by Robert Moll. The feet are painted nails, toothpicks, or cocktail forks. (Photograph by the artist)

Another Robert Moll work. The stones here are polished oriental garden stones found on the beach at Rockaway. The eyes are all brass lamp parts, washers, and such; noses, artist's pen points. (Photograph by the artist)

The symmetry of this painted owl's eyes is emphasized by an asymmetrical body. (Jerry Philips, artist and photograph)

Marion McChesney's *Cliff Dwellers* are time-consuming but fun to create. She uses endcuts of butternut or black walnut, gluing the pieces together under extreme pressure. This forces the glue to run down and create added interest to the background. The variety of stones, backgrounds, and groupings for the Cliff Dwellers is almost infinite.

The base of this owl tree is made of self-hardening clay which makes it possible to really embed the owls. If you use gray clay it will harden to the texture and color of a stone. (Evelyn Meier, artist)

Here's a large family of very colorful owls. The bodies are a bright green with touches of yellow, orange, and white. (Charles Daugherty and Don Coppola, artists)

These owls are painted in beautiful earth tones which contrast strikingly with the white eyes and chests. Each owl nests on a craggy stone. (Evelyn Meier, artist)

Jean Kawecki combines a lovely natural green mineral stone with oxidized copper for the face and wings (for details of this artist's technique of combining stone and copper see Chapter 5).

You might call this a collage owl since it is made up of many different stones: The body is a naturally owl-shaped flat brown stone. The beak is a curved brown stone. The eyes are two round stones painted white, with small brown pebbles glued on as pupils. The feathers are made up of lots of yellowish-brown pebbles heaped all around the body. The owl is mounted on a large piece of mica.

Meet "The Smiths," Arline Shapiro's owl family combined into a wall hanging with bits of weathered wood. The owl stones are all natural formations with just touches of pen and ink to emphasize features.

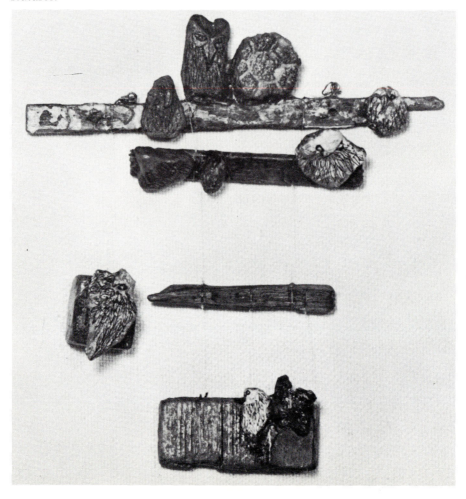

SOURCES OF SUPPLIES

Practically all of the materials mentioned in this book are available in art, hardware, and hobby supply stores throughout the country. In case you have difficulty in locating anything, following is a list of manufacturers to whom you can write for information about retail outlets near you, and suppliers who will fill small retail orders by mail. There are many other fine and useful products and this list is by no means all-inclusive or intended as an exclusive endorsement.

Acrylic Paints, Mediums, and Gesso

Hyplar
M. Grumbacher, Inc.
460 W. 34th St.
New York, N.Y. 10017

Liquitex
Permanent Pigments, Inc.
2700 Highland Avenue
Cincinnati, Ohio 45212

Adhesives

Duco Cement
E. I. du Pont de Nemours & Co.
Wilmington, Del. 19898

Elmer's Glue-All
Borden Inc.
New York, N.Y. 10017

Five Minute Epoxy
Devcon Corporation
Danvers, Mass. 09923

PC 7 Epoxy
Protective Coating Co.
South Basin
Allentown, Pa.

Quick
Slomon Labs, Inc.
32-45 Hunters Point Avenue
New York, N.Y. 10010

Arts and Crafts Mail Order Suppliers, Miscellaneous

American Handicrafts
(See phone book for address nearest you)

Dick Blick
P.O. Box 1268
Galesburg, Ill. 61401

Economy Handicrafts
47-11 Francis Lewis Blvd.
Flushing, N.Y. 11363

Bookends, Unfinished

Economy Handicrafts
47-11 Francis Lewis Blvd.
Flushing, N.Y. 11363
(See catalog)

Casting Resin

California Titan Products, Inc.
320 E. Alton St.
Santa Ana, Calif. 92707

Decoupage Prints, Black and White

Elyse Sommer
Box E
Woodmere, N.Y. 11598
(Illustrated flier, 50c)

Eggs

Julia Hernberg (goose eggs)
1702 Cornwallis Pkway
Cape Coral, Fla. 33904
(Stamped, addressed envelope)

Sources of Supply for Eggers

Kit Stansbury
411 Warren Street
Phillipsburg, N.J. 08865
($1)

Enamel, Polymer

Boss Gloss
California Titan Products, Inc.
320 E. Alton St.
Santa Ana, Calif. 92707

Jewelry Findings and Supplies

Jewelart, Inc.
P.O. Box 9
Tarzana, Calif. 91536
(Catalog 35c)

Sy Schweitzer & Co., Inc.
P.O. Box 431
East Greenwich, R.I. 02818
(Catalog 35c)

Lead Came and Other Stained Glass Supplies

Artist and Craftsman Guild
17 Eastman St.
Cranford, N.J. 07016

Stained Glass Club
482 Tappan Road
Northvale, N.J.

Plastic Spray

Klear-Kote
American Handicrafts
(See phone book for address nearest you)

Krylon
Norristown, Pa.

Plexiglass Stands, Cubes, Etc.

Amplast
359 Canal Street
New York, N.Y. 10013

Mail Order Plastics
58 Lispenard St.
New York, N.Y. 10013

Polymer Enamels
See Enamel, polymer

Resin Casting Supplies
See Casting Resin

Solder and Soldering Irons
See Lead Came

Stewart Clay Co.
133 Mulberry St.
New York, N.Y. 10022

Styrofoam

Dennison's Party Bazaar
390 Fifth Avenue
New York, N.Y. 10018

Economy Handicrafts
47-11 Francis Lewis Blvd.
Flushing, N.Y. 11363

Velcro

Home-Sew, Inc.
1825 West Market St.
Bethlehem, Pa. 18018

Velcro Corporation
681 Fifth Avenue
New York, N.Y. 10022

INDEX

A
Abstract pebble collage, 43
Alternatives to painting, 22–31
Arnel, Jeanie, 57
Assemblage, 39–46

B
Benes, Barton, 33, 59
Blum, Motke, 69
Bookends, 36
Bookmarks, 35
Bonsais, 83, 84
Bread dough, 34

C
Casting resin, embedding stones in, 16, 17
Chess sets, 60, 61
Cloisonné enamel on stone, 28, 29
Cohen, Cindy, 56
Collage
   assemblage and, 43
   decoupage and, 44
   owl, 92
   table, 37, 38
Coppola, Don, 21, 34, 35, 56, 72, 79, 90

D
Daugherty, Charles, 21, 34, 35, 56, 72, 79, 90
Deaton, Jean, 26
Decoupage, 22, 23, 29, 37, 44
Display ideas, 14–21
Doorstops, 33, 34

E
Eggs, decorated with pebbles, 80–82

F
Fine, Cecile, 44, 45

G
Gary, Jan, 20, 58
Gorman, William, 55, 60, 61
Greeting cards, 79, 80

H
Hernberg, Julia, 81, 82
Holiday projects, 78–85

J
Jewelry
   belt, 73

bolos, 73
bracelets, 73
findings, 70
key holder, 73
leaded stones, 74–76
macramé, 74
necklace and earrings, 71
pins, 72
rings, 71, 72

K
Kawecki, Jean, 47, 48, 49, 91

L
Le Norrey, Charles, 4, 13, 36
Leaded stones, 75

M
Macramé-look necklace, 74
McChesney, Marion, 45, 46, 88
Meier, Evelyn, 19, 89, 91
Moll, Robert, 87
Mosaics
    embedded in cement, 67–69
    embedded in Styrofoam, 65–67
    on slate and wood, 65

N
Necklaces and pendants, 71–77
Newsome, Arden J., 56, 72, 86

O
Ogino, Yashikazo, 14
Owls, 86–92

P
Painting
    accessories, 9
    alternatives to, 22–31
    basic techniques, 10, 11
    brushes, 8
    color information, 7, 8
    display ideas for, 14–21
    history of rock painting, 7
    pen and marker painting, 9

Pebble portraits, 39–41
Philips, Jerry, 11, 53–55, 8
Printing on stones, 29

R
Resin-embedded stones, 15–16
Rock hunting, 5, 6
Rosenthal, Carol Lynn, 21, 35, 57, 78, 79, 86

S
Schacter, Justine R., 18, 41, 42, 73
Scully, Frances, 13
Sculpture
    humorous, 51, 52
    natural stone, 48–51
    plexiglass and stone, 53–55
    soapstone, 62, 63
    wire and stone, 57
Shapiro, Arline, 39, 41, 59, 60, 92
Slate
    bookshelf-pencil holder, 34, 35
    clock, 36, 37
    enameling on, 27–29
    etching on, 30–32
    stenciling on, 24
    tissue collage slate table, 37, 38
Sommer, Joellen, 24, 25
Sommer, Mike, 6, 18, 33, 49, 50
Stenciling, 24, 25
Stribling, Mary Lou, 77

T
Tissue collage, 37
Trifon, Harriette, 17, 33, 57

V
Vaeth, Susan, 12, 17, 36, 72, 80
Vogel, Walter, 27, 29, 72, 86

W
Weber, Dee, 40
Weiner, Kay, 66–68
Whales, 21, 53–55